AMERICA
THE JEWISH EXPERIENCE

Sondra Leiman

Jonathan D. Sarna, Consulting Editor

UAHC Press
New York, New York

Library of Congress Cataloging-in-Publication Data

Leiman, Sondra. America: the Jewish experience/by Sondra Leiman;
Jonathan D. Sarna, consulting editor.
p.   cm.
Includes bibliographical references.
ISBN 0-8074-0500-0

1.Jews—United States—History—Juvenile literature. 2. Immigrants—United
States—History—Juvenile literature. 3. Judaism—United States—History—
Juvenile literature. 4. United States—Ethnic relations—Juvenile literature.
[1. Jews—United States—History. 2. Judaism. 3.Ethnic relations.]
I. Sarna, Jonathan D. II. Title.

E184.J5L57226 1993
973'.04924—dc20
93-4647 CIP AC

ACKNOWLEDGMENTS

I sincerely hope that all of the students who read this book will derive as much enjoyment from it as I had writing it. I am deeply grateful to the Maurice Amado Foundation, whose generous support made this book possible. I am also indebted to SAR Academy, Riverdale, New York, for granting me a sabbatical that enabled me to begin the project.

There are many people who encouraged me with their wisdom and insight. First, I would like to thank my consulting editor, Dr. Jonathan Sarna of Brandeis University, under whose watchful eye and tutelage this book took shape. I would also like to thank the following people who read one or more chapters of the manuscript and contributed valuable advice: Martha K. Bindeman, Rabbi Howard I. Bogot, Rabbi Jordan Cohen, Robin Eisenberg, Gail Teicher Fellus, Dru Greenwood, Aron Hirt-Manheimer, Dr. Joakim Isaacs, Rabbi Gerald Kane, Rabbi Beth Klafter, Dr. Jacob Rader Marcus, Nachama Skolnik Moskowitz, Dr. Kerry M. Olitzky, Connie R. Reiter, Rabbi Daniel B. Syme, Karen Trager, and Rabbi Bernard M. Zlotowitz. In addition, I wish to thank the many children who read parts of the manuscript and shared their reactions. I also extend my gratitude to Kathy Parnass, the book's copy editor who did such fine work polishing the manuscript, and to Lori Stahl, who selected the book's photographs and illustrations. Special thanks go to Stuart Benick and Seymour Rossel for carefully guiding the book to final publication.

In addition, I want to acknowledge the people whose memoirs and anecdotes form the basis of the stories that are included in this book. My thanks to Bernard Marinbach, author of *Galveston, Ellis Island of the West* (SUNY Press), who inspired the story "By Boat to Galveston, Texas"; to Joseph Papo, author of *Sephardim of the Twentieth Century* (Pele Yoetz Books), whose anecdote about the Jews of Seattle inspired "The Jewish Fishermen"; to Judith Kaplan Eisenstein, whose story "No Thunder Sounded, No Lightning Struck," which originally appeared in *Eyewitnesses to American Jewish History* (UAHC Press), I edited for a younger audience; to the American Jewish Archives in Cincinnati for providing me with information that inspired the story "One Fateful Night"; to Janice Rothschild Blumberg, whose autobiographical book *One Voice: Rabbi Jacob M. Rothschild and the Troubled South* (Mercer University Press) inspired the story "This Time It Was Different."

David P. Kasakove, my editor, has been the support beam of this entire venture. Whenever I needed help and encouragement, David was always there for me.

I also want to thank my husband, Raymond, for his love and willingness to read each section of the manuscript as it was being written. —SONDRA LEIMAN

The publication of this book
has been made possible through
the generous support of the
Maurice Amado Foundation

PICTURE CREDITS

American Jewish Archives: pp. 37, 41, 46, 58, 68, 69, 73, 74, 77, 95, 113, 128, 149

American Jewish Historical Society: pp. 19, 21, 97

American Numismatic Society: p. 85

Architect of the Capitol, Collection of the House of Representatives: p. 34

Archives of Isaac M. Wise Temple: p. 70

Atlanta Historical Center: p. 169

Baseball Hall of Fame: p. 149

Chicago Jewish Archives, Spertus College: p. 149

Columbia Records: p. 179

Congregation Mikveh Israel: p. 38

Congregation Shearith Israel: p. 112

Dan Klores Associates: p. 179

DC Comics: p. 149 (Reprinted from ACTION COMICS #1 © 1939, © renewed 1967 DC Comics. Used by permission.)

Dell Yearling: p. 179

Duestche Grammophone: p. 179

Ewing Galoway, NY: p. 39

FBI Archives: p. 167

Hadassah: p. 133

Jewish Historical Society of Maryland, Inc.: p. 48; p. 54 (In cooperation with Joan Sturhahn)

Jewish Theological Seminary of America: pp. 80, 125, 126

JFK Library: p. 166

Labor Management Documentation Center, Cornell University: pp. 104, 105

Levi Strauss & Company: pp. 59, 60

Library of Congress: p. 136

Mariner's Museum: p. 61

Missouri Historical Society: p. 111

Museum of the City of New York: p. 96 (Jacob A. Riis Collection, photograph by Jessie Tarbox Beals); p.122 (Photograph by Warren Dickerson); p. 141 (International News Photo)

Museum of History and Industry: p. 114

NAACP, National Public Relations: p. 164

National Archives: p. 142

National Department of Education: p. 174

National Museum of American Jewish History, Philadelphia: p. 78

New York Convention & Visitor's Bureau: pp. 8, 90

New York Public Library: p. 4 (Map Division, Astor, Lenox and Tilden Foundations); pp. 84, 87, 138 (Print Room)

Reform Judaism Magazine: pp. 17, 18, 38, 47, 51, 81, 103, 105, 111, 131, 139, 140, 146, 147, 155, 171, 173, 178, 179, 180

Religious News Service: p. 168

Rhode Island Historical Society: p. 26

Rosenberg Library: p. 101

Smith, Tim: pp. 29, 83, 115, 117, 130, 145, 157

Society of Friends of Touro Synagogue: p. 27

Spiegel, Ted: p. 177

State of Israel Government Press Office: pp. 153, 160

Tony Stone Worldwide: p. 1

UAHC Press: pp. 40, 42, 62 (N. Nodel, artist); pp. 3, 7, 9, 11, 30, 50, 67, 72, 93, 99 (W. Steinel, artist); pp. 36, 56, 66, 79, 108, 109, 123, 132, 154, 165, 167

Wide World Photo: p. 174

Yeshiva University: p. 127

C O N T E N T S

ABOUT YOUR BOOK

Each chapter of your book contains sections that highlight the different parts of the American Jewish experience. Knowing how the chapters are organized will help you gain the most from your studies.

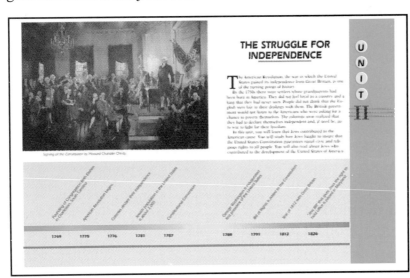

Unit Opener introduces you to different time periods in American Jewish history and previews the material that will be explored in the chapters ahead.

Time Line gives you a quick "snapshot" of the major events that occurred during the time period covered in the unit.

WHAT TO LOOK FOR IN EACH CHAPTER

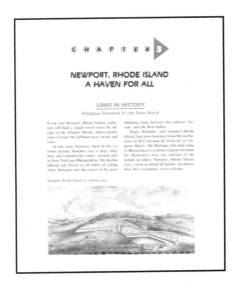

Links in History connects the history of America with the history of American Jews.

The Jewish Experience zeroes in on the unique experiences of Jews during each period of American history.

Fiction and History are combined in each chapter's special story. You will experience history through the lives of the people of a particular time period. The stories are based on letters, diaries, and historic events.

People to Know and **In Their Own Words** introduce you to the lives of some of the most important American Jews. By reading their diaries, letters, and articles, you will get to know what these people felt and thought.

Focus concentrates on one particular aspect of the Jewish experience that is especially important, such as Jewish customs, careers, and immigration.

Checkup helps you review your study of each chapter.

Photographs and Illustrations let you see for yourself the sights and personalities of each period.

I N T R O D U C T I O N

JEWISH BEGINNINGS IN THE NEW WORLD

The history you are about to study is the story of the Jewish people in America. It may also be your grandparents' story, your parents' story, and perhaps even your story. You will learn why Jews came to America, how we came here, and what life has been like for Jews in this country.

Our story begins in 1492, when Christopher Columbus set sail in search of a water route to the East Indies. He did not reach the East Indies because the continents of North and South America lay between them and Spain. Columbus, of course, did not know this. When he landed on an island in the Bahamas, he mistakenly thought that he had reached the East Indies. Therefore, he named the Native American people he found there Indians.

THE JEWISH EXPERIENCE

The story of the Jewish people in the Americas also begins in 1492. In that year, the king and queen of Spain, Ferdinand and Isabella, decided to expel the hundreds of thousands of Jews living in their country. Why did these monarchs make this decision? What does the expulsion of the Jews from Spain have to do with Columbus and the history of the Jews in America?

THE HISTORY OF THE SPANISH JEWS

Jews arrived in Spain very early in Spanish history. Some people believe that they came during the period in which the Romans conquered Spain, two thousand years ago, at the time the Second Temple was destroyed. As the centuries passed, the Jewish community grew. Jews from Spain are called **Sephardim**. The Hebrew word *Sepharad* refers to the country of Spain.

Although Catholicism has always been the major religion of Spain, for a period of several hundred years, Muslims ruled that country. These Muslims, called Moors, came from North Africa. At times, the Moors treated the Jews as second-class citizens. At other times, however, the Moors and Jews were friendly and helped one another. Some historians call these years the Golden Age of Spain because of the beautiful poetry and the many philosophical and scientific ideas that were produced during this period.

FORCED CONVERSION

Before long, however, the Catholics reconquered Spain. They wanted everyone to convert to Catholicism. Priests went around the country trying to force people to convert. Those who refused were often killed, or their children were taken away by the Church to be raised as Christians. Many Jews decided to convert in order to save their lives and protect their children.

Although large numbers of Jews were baptized as Catholics, or **Conversos**, which is the name that the Spanish gave these people, many of them did not forget the religion of their birth. Some of these Conversos began to play a dangerous game. To the outside world, they pretended to be Catholics. They went to church and observed the Christian holidays. But they continued to observe Judaism secretly. The Conversos who secretly observed Judaism were called **Marranos** by the Spanish, a term that might mean "pig."

THE INQUISITION

The Catholic priests organized a special police force to spy on the Conversos, which was called the **Inquisition**. If the Inquisition believed that a Converso practiced his or her old religion, it labeled that person a **heretic**, or an unbeliever. Such people would be arrested and tortured until they admitted that they had continued to observe Jewish laws.

Those people who could not prove their innocence, as well as those who asserted their belief in Judaism, were burned at the stake. Executions were grand public events, attended by government officials, priests, and townspeople. Often other Conversos were forced to attend. The Spanish name for the burning of a heretic was **auto-de-fé**.

Ferdinand and Isabella were convinced that all Conversos were heretics. Prompted by the chief inquisitor, Tomás de Torquemada, the rulers declared that all Jews be expelled from Spain and allowed the Jews less than five months to leave the country. The final expulsion date was August 2, 1492.

LEAVING SPAIN On August 3, 1492, when Columbus left the harbor of Palos, he and his crew witnessed an incredible scene. Thousands of Jews were boarding all kinds of boats, fleeing Spain. Those Jews who could not get passage aboard a boat fled by land to Portugal, a neighbor of Spain. But a few years later, Portugal, too, expelled its Jews.

NEW HOMES Jews settled in such places as Holland, Turkey, Greece, and North Af-rica. Many Conversos journeyed to colonies that Spain and Portugal had established in the Caribbean, in Central America, and in South America. Many of them hoped to practice Judaism in secret. But the Inquisition, with its auto-de-fés, soon followed the Conversos to the colonies.

One Portuguese colony that attracted Conversos was Recife in Brazil. In 1630, Recife was captured by the Dutch, who permitted Jews to practice their faith openly. In 1654, after a long battle, Recife again fell into Portuguese hands. Its Jews had to flee once more. In the next chapter, you will learn how some of these Jews found their way to New Amsterdam, which became the first Jewish community in North America.

Thousands of Jews left Spain by ship on the same day that Columbus set sail for North America.

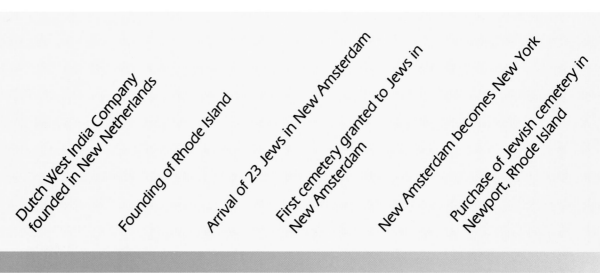

Dutch West India Company founded in New Netherlands	Founding of Rhode Island	Arrival of 23 Jews in New Amsterdam	First cemetery granted to Jews in New Amsterdam	New Amsterdam becomes New York	Purchase of Jewish cemetery in Newport, Rhode Island
1621	**1636**	**1654**	**1656**	**1664**	**1677**

SETTLING IN THE AMERICAN COLONIES

Small groups of Jews settled in the American colonies between 1654 and 1775. Many of them were Sephardim who had fled the Inquisition. There were also adventurous Jews from Germany and other parts of Europe. They left because of laws in their countries that discriminated against Jews. Jews from these areas are called **Ashkenazim**.

Most Jews settled in the port cities of New York, Charleston, Savannah, Newport, and Philadelphia. A major occupation of these early settlers was trading and supplying the British army with basic goods, almost all of which had to be imported. Some colonial Jews gained enough wealth to buy ships that brought goods from England, Holland, and the West Indies.

In this unit, you will learn about the Jews who settled in New Amsterdam, later called New York, and about the Jewish community in Newport, Rhode Island. You will read how hard it was for these Jews to be recognized as citizens and to keep their traditions.

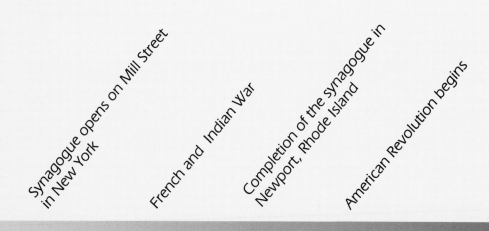

Synagogue opens on Mill Street in New York	French and Indian War	Completion of the synagogue in Newport, Rhode Island	American Revolution begins
1730	1754-1763	1763	1775

NEW AMSTERDAM
AN UNWELCOME START

LINKS IN HISTORY

New Netherlands—A Dutch Colony

New Netherlands, a colony in North America, was supported by the Dutch West India Company, a business group in Holland. New Netherlands included the trading post of New Amsterdam on the island of Manhattan and spread north along the Hudson River valley to Fort Orange. Fort Orange is now called Albany. The company's Dutch stockholders, some of whom were Jews, helped the colony grow, in return for profits. The colonists sent the company furs and other raw materials to sell in Holland.

The governor of New Netherlands was a sharp-tongued man, Peter Stuyvesant.

Stuyvesant had many prejudices. He did not like Jews and Catholics. In fact, he disliked any people who did not worship the way he did. He wanted newcomers to be like the majority of the Dutch citizens, who were called **burghers**.

In 1664, a fleet of British ships appeared in the harbor, ready to take control of the colony. Peter Stuyvesant wanted to fight the British, but the citizens of New Amsterdam refused. As a result, New Amsterdam became the colony of New York, named after the Duke of York, a brother of the English king.

THE JEWISH EXPERIENCE

Imagine how you would feel if you moved to a strange country and found that you were not welcome. In fact, you were so disliked that whenever you tried to claim your rights as a citizen, you were told to pack up and leave.

This was what happened to the first group of Jews who settled in America in the Dutch colony of New Amsterdam in 1654. In that year, twenty-three Jews sailed into the harbor of New Amsterdam aboard a French ship, the *Sainte Catherine*. Their voyage had begun many months before in Recife, Brazil.

FLEEING ONCE AGAIN Owned by the Dutch since 1630, Recife was a lovely town in which Jews lived freely. Many of the people living there had come from Holland. Others had been there since the days of Portuguese rule. Like Holland, Recife was a place where Jews could practice their religion without fear and where families could make a good living. But in 1654, Recife was again conquered by the Portuguese. At this time, the Portuguese, who were Catholics, persecuted people of other religions. Jews and Protestants living in Recife were given three months to make a choice: convert to Catholicism or leave the colony. Because the Jews did not want to become Conversos, they chose to leave Recife.

Some Jews boarded ships for Amsterdam, Holland, where they had family and

Many Jews fled Spain and resettled in the Dutch-owned colony of Recife. When Portugal conquered Recife in 1654, the Jews were expelled. One small group of 23 Jews set out for New Amsterdam.

Since the first 23 Jews arrived in New Amsterdam in 1654, the Jewish population in New York has grown to almost 2 million people.

business connections. Others moved north to settlements along the Atlantic coast in present-day Suriname and the West Indies. And one small group set out for New Amsterdam. It is believed that the members of this group were captured by pirates, who took their ship and left them stranded on a Caribbean island. They were rescued from this island by a French ship bound for New Amsterdam.

SETTLING IN NEW AMSTERDAM After much difficulty, the Jewish immigrants settled in New Amsterdam. The Jewish community remained small for many years. Some of the original settlers left because they found that making a living was too difficult. But before long, new waves of immigrants joined those who had stayed. Today, New York is home to one of the world's largest Jewish communities.

A New Beginning

September in New York can be beautiful. The sun shines brightly. The treetops start showing just a glint of the beautiful reds and yellows that will cover the trees later in the fall. The light breezes wash the air clean of the heavy humidity of summer.

On just such a September day in 1654, a French ship, the *Sainte Catherine*, sailed into the busy harbor of New Amsterdam, the Dutch trading colony founded on the shores of the Hudson River. This was ten years before the town was taken over by the English and renamed New York.

On board the ship was a cargo of much-needed goods, including sugar, rum, molasses, and dyes for cloth. The ship had come from the West Indies, where all of these items were available.

The *Sainte Catherine* carried an additional cargo that was different from that of the other ships being unloaded. This cargo consisted of twenty-three "poor but healthy" men, women, and children. The captain, Jacques de la Mothe, out of the goodness of his heart but also perhaps with an eye to making a large sum of money, had taken them aboard at one of his island stops.

"Pardon me, Captain," Asser Levy, the spokesperson of the group, said quietly, "when can my people leave the ship?"

"My good sir," the captain replied, "you may leave the ship, but you must remain on the dock until your future is settled. There is the matter of the considerable fare to be paid, and you do not have a permit to enter New Amsterdam."

The group stood anxiously on the dock, not knowing what to do. Suddenly, out of the crowd of longshoremen unloading the cargo, a man with a kind face stepped forward.

"*Shalom Alechem*. Peace be unto you," the man said softly. "I understand that you are Jews. My name is Jacob Bar Simson."

No words could have been more welcome to the tired travelers. They all started talking at once, until one of the men raised his hand and signaled for quiet.

"Please," he said, "let us introduce ourselves properly. My name is Asser Levy, and these people are my family and friends. We come here in peace after a hard journey."

"Where did you come from?" Jacob asked.

"We left Recife, Brazil, more than four months ago, but not on this ship. The ship we sailed on was captured by pirates. We were put ashore on a Caribbean island. The good captain saved us. But now we must pay him. Since the pirates took our money, we have only some goods left that we can perhaps sell. But forgive me. I do not mean to burden you with our problems. It is just that we are very excited to find a fellow Jew here. Is there a community of Jews? Is there a group to whom we can appeal for help?"

Jacob Bar Simson shook his head. "No," he said, "there is only one other Jew here, Solomon Pieterson. I myself only arrived three weeks ago from Holland. The governor, Peter Stuyvesant, is a difficult man. From what I hear, he does not want Jews in his colony. I have already written to the Dutch West India Company in Amsterdam, asking permission to stay. It is this company that makes it possible for New Amsterdam to exist by supplying it with extra money when it is needed. We will write another letter and send it off on the next ship. There are Jewish stockholders in the Dutch West India Company. Surely our fellow Jews in Amsterdam will persuade the other stockholders to convince Peter Stuyvesant to grant us permits."

"Good gentlemen," the captain interrupted, "that may happen in the future, but where is the money to pay your fare now?"

The group fell silent. They knew that they had to solve this problem first.

"Do you have any valuables among your goods?" asked Jacob Bar Simson. "I will take them to the auction house and try to sell them to pay your fare."

The twenty-three people gathered what valuables they had and Bar Simson left for the auction house. When he returned, he gave the money he had gotten to the captain, but it was not enough to pay the fare.

Jacob Bar Simson had another plan. "When we write to the Dutch West India Company, we will also write to the Jewish community in Amsterdam," he said. "It is the obligation of Jews everywhere to help one another. Surely they will send us the money that we need."

Meanwhile, the captain was losing his patience. "Enough of this," he shouted. "I brought you here in good faith, and I demand my money now."

"Constable," the captain addressed the policeman who was guarding the group, "put these two men in jail until the money is paid." He pointed to David Israel and Moses Lumbroso.

Suddenly, the group heard a man shout, "What is going on here?" The questioner was none other than the governor, Peter Stuyvesant. Having been told that a strange group of people had just landed, he had come down to the wharf to see for himself.

"Bar Simson, who are these people?" he demanded, having recognized Jacob.

"Sir," Jacob replied, "they are Jews from Recife, who have made their way here with much difficulty. They are asking for permission to settle."

"Settle? Didn't I tell you three weeks ago that I do not want Jews here? That means you and whomever else you bring. There is no place for Jews in our colony. Jews will only become a burden to us. New Amsterdam is a small trading community. Life here is difficult, and we do not want strangers in our midst."

He stamped his wooden leg and thundered, "Be off with you!"

Asser Levy now stepped forward. "Sir,

Jacob Bar Simson did not bring us. We mean no harm. Fate has left us on your doorstep. If we may be permitted to stay here, I assure you that we will be industrious members of the community and do our share to promote its well-being. To this end, we will write to the stockholders of the Dutch West India Company, asking for permission to stay."

"Go ahead, write letters. I will also write to them," Peter Stuyvesant thundered. "There will be no Jews in our colony."

And so the letter-writing campaign began. Stuyvesant wrote that he did not want "hateful, poor" Jews in New Amsterdam.

In the meantime, the captain and his crew decided that the Jews could be trusted to pay the rest of the fare in the future. As a result, David Israel and Moses Lumbroso were released.

The stockholders of the Dutch West India Company replied: "Peter Stuyvesant, you have no permission to turn away these Jews. They were loyal citizens of Holland in our Dutch colony of Recife. They have met with hardship. Let them settle among you, and allow them to earn a living."

After Peter Stuyvesant received the letter, he met with the Jews. He said, "I have been commanded to permit you to live in New Amsterdam. What guarantee do I have that you will be able to take care of yourselves?"

"Sir," Asser Levy replied, "if you grant us the right to work, we will support ourselves. In the event that some of us will need help, we will write to the Jews of Amsterdam. It is a religious obligation that Jews help one another."

Peter Stuyvesant reluctantly permitted the Jews to settle in New Amsterdam. But

that was not the end of the matter. He made it difficult for them to earn a living. He rejected their petition to hold religious services in their homes. When the settlers asked for permission to stand guard duty, he refused and ordered them to pay a tax instead.

The Dutch West India Company rebuked Governor Stuyvesant: "We are displeased that you have forbidden the Jews to trade, carry on business, and buy land. From now on, you must obey our orders in this matter."

Asser Levy and his friends read the letter from the Dutch West India Company with great joy. "And read this," Asser said happily. "It says that we are also allowed to stand guard duty and hold religious services. At last, we are on our way to becoming full citizens."

IN THEIR OWN WORDS

A Jewish Petition to the Governors of New Amsterdam

It took more than two and a half years for the Jews of New Amsterdam to become citizens with full rights in the Dutch colony. Here is an excerpt from the petition that the Jews presented to the governing council of New Amsterdam.

> We, the undersigned, of the Jewish Nation here, make known with due reverence how that one of our Nation [Asser Levy] repaired to the City Hall of this City and requested of the Noble Burgomasters that he might obtain his Burgher [citizenship] certificate, like other Burghers, which to our great surprise was declined and refused by the Noble Burgomasters.
>
> We, therefore, reverently request your Noble Worships to please not exclude nor shut us out from the Burgher right, but to notify the Noble Burgomasters that they should . . . give us the customary Burgher certificate. . . .
>
> Below stood: Your Noble Worships Jacob Cohen Henricques, Abraham de Lucena, Joseph d'Acosta.

F O C U S

THE FIRST CEMETERY OF THE JEWISH COMMUNITY OF NEW YORK

When Jews move to a new place, they must make sure that they take care of certain needs in order to establish a religious community. You might assume that the most important community need is the founding of a synagogue. Although a synagogue is high on the list, it is not usually the first priority. The reason is that a *minyan,* made up of ten Jews, can come together anywhere for a prayer service if no synagogue building is available. Tradition teaches us that a school is more important than a synagogue. Why do you think this is?

A Jewish cemetery is also at the top of the list. Jews do not want to be buried in a cemetery that belongs to people of another religion. In 1656, several members of the Jewish community in the colony of New York petitioned the town council for land for a cemetery. The council agreed and "point[ed] out to the petitioners a little hook of land situate[d] outside of this city for a burial place. . . . " The whereabouts of this first cemetery are not known today.

In 1682, the Jewish community of New York purchased a new piece of ground for a cemetery. A small part of this cemetery still remains nestled among the tall buildings of lower Manhattan, in the shadow of the World Trade Center.

C H A P T E R **1** ▶ CHECKUP

WORD BANK

Inquisition	Holland	Recife
Marranos	Sephardim	Burghers
Asser Levy	New York	Dutch West India Company
	Fort Orange	Conversos

Use the **Word Bank** to complete the following sentences.

1. The twenty-three Jewish travelers were fleeing from _____, Brazil.

2. The _____ was a special police force that persecuted secret Jews.

3. The _____ was a business company in _____ that ordered Peter Stuyvesant to permit Jews to reside in New Amsterdam.

4. This person won the right to stand guard duty and petitioned to become a citizen of New Amsterdam. His name is _____.

5. New Amsterdam became the British colony of _____, named after the brother of the English king.

6. Albany, New York, was originally called _____.

7. Jews who secretly practiced Judaism in Spain and Portugal were called _____.

8. _____ were Jews who were pressured into being baptized as Catholics.

9. Jews from Spain and Portugal are called _____.

10. The Jews of New Amsterdam petitioned for the right to become citizens or _____.

DISCUSSION

The story in this chapter illustrates the following important Jewish value: "All Israel is responsible for one another." How would you handle the following situations?

A. Imagine that Jews living in a foreign land were suddenly forced to leave their country. These Jews are now immigrating to the United States, as well as to Israel. Many communities have been asked to help. Your temple has volunteered to be responsible for a dozen Jewish families. Pretend that you are in charge of organizing this effort. How would you plan your strategy? Remember that the members of these families need housing, food, clothes, and jobs they can do. Some of them may also need medical services. Use the chart below to plan your strategy.

	SOCIAL ACTION PLAN
Housing	
Food	
Clothes	
Jobs	
Medical services	

B. A homeless Jewish person has approached you and your family for help. How would you go about helping that person?

ACTIVITIES

1. Pretend that you were a passenger on the *Sainte Catherine*. The captain is a kind man, but he now wishes to be paid. The pirates have taken your money but not your possessions. The captain wants these as payment.

Make a list of ten precious Jewish religious objects that you will need in the New World in order to live a Jewish life. Decide what you would be willing to give to the captain and what you cannot part with. Since all the items on your list are important for Jewish living, tell how you might go about replacing them in the near future. Compare your list with those of your classmates and discuss your ideas.

a. _____   **f.** _____

b. _____   **g.** _____

c. _____   **h.** _____

d. _____   **i.** _____

e. _____   **j.** _____

2. Write and act out a short skit dramatizing the scene between Asser Levy and Peter Stuyvesant in which Asser asks the governor to allow the twenty-three Jews from Recife to stay in New Amsterdam.

3. Write a letter to Peter Stuyvesant, asking for the right to settle in New Amsterdam. Tell him of your intention to be a good citizen and take part in the affairs of the community.

To Peter Stuyvesant, Governor:

Sincerely,

15

C H A P T E R 2

NEW YORK
ROOTS OF A GREAT COMMUNITY

LINKS IN HISTORY

A British Colony

By the early 1700s, New York City had changed from a Dutch-speaking town to a small British-ruled city with many cultures. The settlers were from many nations and practiced many religions.

The colony of New York included more than the city of New York. It extended north along the shores of the Hudson River and west around the Finger Lakes. Native Americans living on these lands supplied the colonists with fur pelts.

New York City had a fine harbor. The colonists used the harbor to export and import goods. In those early days, the residents of British New York were proud of their way of life. The farmers of the colony of New York were happy that they owned their land. The traders were pleased with their businesses. As subjects of the British king, both groups enjoyed the same rights as the English people.

THE JEWISH EXPERIENCE

The Jewish citizens of New York in the 1700s were not all Spanish and Portuguese, as the first Jewish inhabitants of New Amsterdam had been. Now there were also Jews from England, Holland, and France, as well as Poland, Hungary, and Germany. However, New York still only had a Jewish population of a few hundred people.

TRADE Jews were actively engaged in trading and shipping. They traveled to the frontier posts to buy furs from the Native Americans. Much of their daily business, however, was carried on in the busy harbor area. Jewish-owned ships arrived with iron goods, furniture, and fine cloth—as well as tea and mail—from England. From the West Indies, vessels brought rum and sugar. They

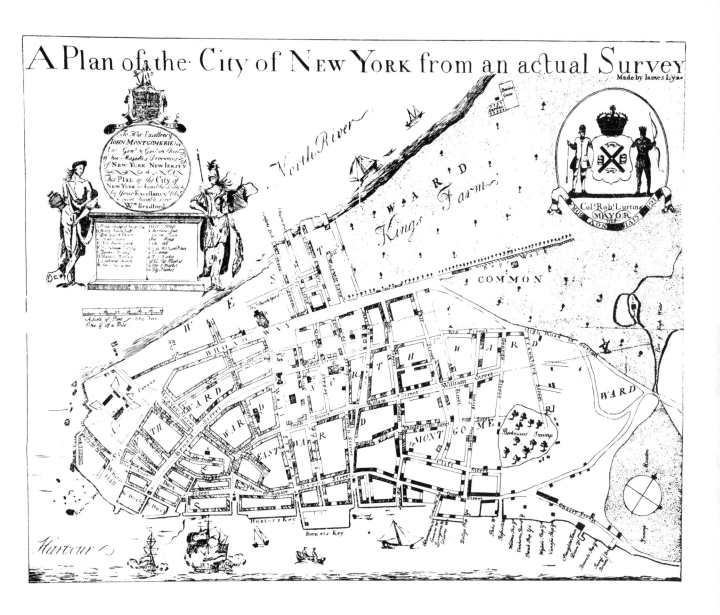

left New York loaded with furs and wheat. Leading Jewish merchants included Mordecai Gomez, Jacob Franks, and Moses Levy.

SYNAGOGUE LIFE   The Jewish community rented a house near the waterfront on Beaver Street, where they held services. As you read in the last chapter, they already owned a cemetery. Believing that all Jews are responsible for one another, they wrote to the wealthier Jewish community of Jamaica in the West Indies for a donation to build a synagogue and erect a fence around the cemetery. Financial help soon arrived, and in 1730, the community built a synagogue on Mill Street.

17

Although there were no rabbis in the colonies in those days, there were many educated people who volunteered their services to the synagogue. A person who had both a knowledge of Judaism and a good voice was given the position of **chazan**. The *chazan* planned the services and taught the children.

Since there were no public schools, children attended private schools. The Jewish school was run by the synagogue on Mill Street. The teacher was paid by the parents. If parents could not pay, their children were given a free education. Parents wanted their children to learn Hebrew, Spanish, and English in the school. Spanish was taught because the sermon and rituals were still based on the culture of the Jewish Spanish-Portuguese settlers of New Amsterdam.

The synagogue on Mill Street in New Amsterdam was the first Jewish house of worship in the colonies.

SEPHARDIM AND ASHKENAZIM We have learned that Sephardim originally came from Spain and Portugal. Although they were expelled from those countries, they maintained their customs. In colonial America, some of them continued to speak Portuguese and Spanish, as well as English. They built their synagogues in the Sephardic style. The *bimah* was in the middle of the room. The congregation sat on benches around the *bimah*.

By 1740, however, the majority of the Jews in the colonies were Ashkenazim. Ashkenazim are Jews whose origins are in Northern, Central, and Eastern Europe, particularly Germany and Poland. Ashkenazim and Sephardim follow certain customs, both at home and in the synagogue. The Ashkenazim who came to the colonies

seem to have found Sephardic rituals and customs appealing. They followed local custom and became members of the established Sephardic synagogues.

CITIZENS OF THE NEW WORLD In 1686, the British declared that "all persons of what religion soever" may practice freely. The Jews of New York felt very much at home by then, even though they had not yet won all the privileges that the majority of the population enjoyed. They had their synagogue, a cemetery, and a school and were accepted as merchants and traders.

In 1711, seven leading Jewish families contributed money to help their Christian neighbors complete the building of a church. Different groups of people in the colonies were learning to respect one another. They recognized that giving created a feeling of community. The road ahead was not going to be easy, but the goal of a new, freer way of life was within reach.

Letters to Naphtali

Jacob Franks was a prosperous merchant and shipper who lived in the colony of New York. He was the son of a well-to-do English Jewish family that had immigrated to New York in the early 1700s. Jacob supplied the British soldiers in New York during the French and Indian War with clothes and food, as well as guns and ammunition. In those days, soldiers received their supplies from private merchants.

Abigail, a pious Jewish woman, had come from London, England, with her father, Moses Levy. Moses Levy was a successful merchant.

He had given his clever daughter an excellent education in London. She had read many novels and had seen all the best plays.

Not long after the Levys arrived, Abigail met Jacob Franks. Their marriage was successful. They had three children: Naphtali, Phila, and Rachel. They were both active members of the synagogue on Mill Street. At one time, Jacob was the president. Abigail organized many of the synagogue's charitable activities. All was well in the Franks household except for one very big disappointment. That is what the following story is about.

Abigail sat at her writing table for a long time. She was trying to compose a letter to her son, Naphtali. Naphtali lived in London, where he managed the family's business, trading goods imported from the colonies. Her husband, Jacob Franks, had been in Albany for a month now, selling supplies to the British officers stationed at that northern outpost.

It had been a very difficult time for Abigail. The summer's humidity hung heavily around the family's elegant New York mansion. Abigail found her many duties—which included managing her large home, preparing for Rosh Hashanah and Yom Kippur, and overseeing her husband's numerous business affairs in his absence—especially difficult in the hot days of the waning summer.

But all of these hardships paled compared with the events of the last week. Her

Abigail Franks, painted around 1740.

elder daughter, Phila, a headstrong twenty-year-old girl, was missing. Phila had left the house to go to the market several days before and had not returned. Everyone had looked for Phila—Abigail, sixteen-year-old Rachel, the servants, the constables—but to no avail.

The neighbors had tried to help, but they only increased Abigail's sense of foreboding. They whispered that perhaps Phila had run away with an admirer. Phila was very beautiful, and there were many young men who sought her hand in marriage. Her mother was afraid that something terrible had happened to her impulsive daughter.

As Abigail thought about how she was going to describe the events of the past few days to her son, there was a knock on her door.

"Who is it?" asked Abigail.

"It's I, Mother," answered Rachel, walking slowly into the room.

"Rachel, what is the matter?" Abigail asked, as she looked at her younger daughter, a pretty sixteen-year-old. "You are so pale. Do you have any word of Phila?"

Rachel remained silent.

"Oh, Rachel, you do know something. Out with it. You know how anxious I am for some news!"

"Mother, I know where she is. I know where Phila has gone," Rachel replied, hardly daring to look at her mother.

"Where, dear, where has she gone?" Abigail stood up from her writing table, the letter to Naphtali momentarily forgotten.

"Mrs. Lucena says that she saw her today near the wharf and spoke with her."

"Spoke with her! Why didn't Rebecca Lucena come and tell me this herself? What did your sister say to her? Rachel, tell me! Oh, my dear, why do you hesitate?"

"Please, Mother, sit down and I will tell you what Mrs. Lucena said." Rachel guided her mother to the edge of the bed.

"Mrs. Lucena said that when she went down to the wharf this morning to deliver her husband's lunch, she saw Phila going into Oliver DeLancy's office. Mrs. Lucena said to her, 'Phila, where have you been? Your mother is beside herself with worry. The whole community is looking for you.'"

"Please, Rachel, get to the point," her mother interrupted. "What did Phila say?"

"Mother, she is married! She has gone and married Oliver DeLancy!"

Abigail Frank looked at her youngest child and began to weep. "Oh, no," she cried, shaking Rachel. "Tell me that it isn't true. How could she marry out of our faith? Your father will be so upset. He has tried to teach all of you the beauty of Judaism and the importance of passing down its practices from one generation to the next."

"I know, Mother, but what can we do?" Rachel put her arms around her mother to comfort her. "Everyone is talking about it by now, if I know Mrs. Lucena. She can't keep a thing to herself."

"Perhaps your father will know what to do," said Abigail, "but in the meantime, tell the servants that I do not wish to be disturbed. I can't bear to see anyone."

"Mother, please don't stay up here alone. Please come downstairs for dinner."

"No, Rachel, let me be. I cannot face anyone. I am ashamed that a child of ours could be so disobedient. And Rachel, if Phila or her husband should come to the door, I forbid you or the servants to admit them."

After Rachel left, Abigail returned to her writing table. This time, she took the paper on which she was going to write to

Naphtali and tore it up into little pieces.

Another week passed, and Jacob Franks still had not returned from his trip. Abigail once more attempted to write to her son.

"This just will not do," Abigail said to herself as she brushed away tears. "One of Jacob's ships leaves for London at daybreak tomorrow. Naphtali will be very upset if he does not receive a letter. He must hear about his sister's elopement from my pen and not from some gossip."

Dearest Naphtali,

It gives me great joy to hear that your dear son is growing so nicely. May heaven smile on you and your loving wife.

As for me, I am in a state of shock. Your sister Phila has secretly married Oliver DeLancy. Although he comes from a well-known family, he is not of our faith. Would that I had sent her to you in London to find a Jewish husband. Now they come to my door to try to make peace with the family, but I wish to have nothing to do with them. My house has become my prison. I do not have the heart to go into the street.

Your affectionate mother,
Abigail Franks

After Abigail had sent the letter to the ship, she began to feel better. Perhaps it was because it was Friday and she remembered all that she had to do to prepare for the Sabbath. She left her room and busied herself with the household chores. She expected Jacob home soon. How was she going to find the words to tell him what had happened?

Just as she was about to light the Sabbath candles, she heard her husband's car-

Jacob Franks, painted around 1740.

riage rumble into the driveway. As he came into the room, he greeted his wife.

"Abigail, I heard the terrible news while I was upstate," he said. "Please, dear, light the Sabbath candles, and then we will talk."

After Abigail finished reciting the blessing, she put her arm around her husband's shoulder. He sat wearily in his chair, with his head in his hands.

"Oliver DeLancy, the scoundrel! How could Phila do such a thing? We have tried so hard to raise our children to be responsible and observant Jews. And now this."

It was Abigail's turn to console. "I know, Jacob. As much as we try, we cannot control all of the events in our lives. We are

21

proud Jews. We have given our children the best Jewish education that our colony has to offer. You are the president of the synagogue, and we have both spent much time seeing to its welfare. What more can a family do?"

"I know what we have to do," Jacob replied. "We must vow never to see Phila or her husband. She has turned away from our heritage and cannot be a part of our family as long as she is married to that man."

"I have already taken that vow," said Abigail sadly.

"Furthermore," Jacob went on, "we must make sure that this does not happen to Rachel. We will write to Naphtali and ask him if Rachel can go live with him in London. She will finish her education there. We will also ask him to introduce her to a fine Jewish gentleman. We are going to miss her terribly, but we both know that this arrangement is for the best."

Just before Rosh Hashanah, Abigail again wrote to her son.

Dearest Naphtali,

I have overcome my depression, but I have vowed not to see Phila nor let any of the family communicate with her. My neighbors no longer speak of the matter. I am relieved that you will take care of Rachel. She will embark on her journey to London after Sukkot. . . . I conclude with my prayers for your health and happiness this New Year. I am, my dear son,

Your affectionate mother,
Abigail Franks

P.S. On the return boat, please send me a new pair of spectacles.

That Yom Kippur, during the synagogue service, Abigail Franks listened to the *Kol Nidre* prayer, which released the members of the congregation from their vows. She thought of the vows she had made during the past year.

"Perhaps," she thought, "I have been too hasty. I vowed that I would never see Phila again. But if she and Oliver come to my door one more time, I won't turn them away. They will have children someday, and I would like to instruct my grandchildren in the practices of our religion. After services, I will tell Jacob my decision."

At the same time, Jacob Franks, wrapped in his *talit* and listening to the words of *Kol Nidre*, had made the identical decision.

Fill in the spaces in Column A with the correct letters from Column B.

A	B
1. New York ____	**A.** Leading merchant and president of the synagogue on Mill Street
2. Jacob Franks ____	**B.** First synagogue built in the colonies
3. West Indies ____	**C.** Leader of services and a teacher
4. Abigail Franks ____	**D.** Source of rum and sugarcane
5. The synagogue on Mill Street ____	**E.** Outstanding Jewish woman of the colony of New York
6. *Chazan*____	**F.** Formerly New Amsterdam

DISCUSSION

1. Abigail was very disappointed in her daughter Phila. Not only did Abigail refuse to see her daughter, she would not even leave her house or speak to her neighbors. Why did Phila's marriage upset Abigail and Jacob? Why are Jews today concerned about intermarriage?

2. In the story, *Kol Nidre* released Abigail and Jacob from their vows. What does being released from vows mean? Were the Franks right in making their vows? Why do you think they wanted to be released from their vows? Did you ever make a promise that you couldn't keep? Invite your rabbi to class, or have your teacher explain the meaning of *Kol Nidre*.

ACTIVITIES

1. You and a group of people in your community want to start a new synagogue. There are many things to think about. Complete the chart on the next page, using the following headings: Personnel (people you need to hire to run the synagogue), Lay Committees (the different kinds of committees you will need, for example, an education committee, a ritual committee, etc.), Clubs, Methods of Raising Money, Calendar for the Year. Compare your chart with those of your classmates, and make a master chart that contains the best suggestions.

THE ——————————————— SYNAGOGUE

Personnel	Committees	Clubs

Fund-raising methods

_____

_____

_____

CALENDAR OF EVENTS FOR THE YEAR 57_____

Tishri _____   Nisan _____

_____   _____

Cheshvan _____   Iyar _____

_____   _____

Kislev _____   Sivan _____

_____   _____

Tevet _____   Tamuz _____

_____   _____

Shevat _____   Av _____

_____   _____

Adar _____   Elul _____

_____   _____

2. You are in charge of hiring a new *chazan* for your synagogue, who will also be a teacher. Write a list of questions that you will ask to determine if this is the right person for your congregation. Write a list of questions that the *chazan* might ask you about the congregation.

Your Questions

a. _____

b. _____

c. _____

d. _____

e. _____

Chazan's Questions

a. _____

b. _____

c. _____

d. _____

e. _____

3. Draw a picture of early New York. Try to include all of the following:

A busy harbor with many sailing ships; Front Street, which faces the harbor, with its shipping and trading office buildings; Mill Street with its houses, cemetery, and synagogue; Wall Street with the governor's mansion, Trinity Church, and more elegant homes.

Remember, the roads were not yet paved; livestock—chickens, pigs, and cows—roamed about the streets; the wash hung in people's yards to dry; people either walked, rode horses, or used carriages to get about; people shopped in open stalls operated by street venders.

Make your drawing colorful, and label the sights.

NEWPORT, RHODE ISLAND
A HAVEN FOR ALL

LINKS IN HISTORY

Religious Freedom in the New World

If you visit Newport, Rhode Island, today, you will find a small resort town by the edge of the Atlantic Ocean, where people come to enjoy the sailboat races, swim, and relax.

At one time, however, back in the colonial period, Newport was a large shipping and commercial center, second only to New York and Philadelphia. The harbor offered safe haven to all kinds of sailing ships. Newport was the center of the great shipping trade between the colonies, Europe, and the West Indies.

Roger Williams, who founded Rhode Island, had been banished from Massachusetts in 1635 because he believed in religious liberty. The Puritans who had come to Massachusetts seeking religious freedom for themselves were not tolerant of the beliefs of others. Newport, Rhode Island, was a town in which all people, no matter how they worshiped, were welcome.

Newport, Rhode Island, in colonial times.

THE JEWISH EXPERIENCE

Jews flocked to Newport, Rhode Island. In 1677, they purchased ground for a Jewish cemetery. By 1759, the Jewish community of Newport was the second largest in America. Many of its members were Sephardic Jews who had strong ties with other Sephardic communities in America and the West Indies. Some were members of families that practiced Judaism in secret in Portugal.

BUILDING A SYNAGOGUE The leaders of the Newport community decided to build a synagogue. They wrote to their fellow Jews in New York, asking for financial help to construct the building. Peter Harrison, a famous colonial architect, was invited to design the synagogue. Touro Synagogue was completed in 1763. Visitors were astonished by the beauty of the building.

The members of the community served as officers of the synagogue. They set aside time to teach Hebrew to the children. In those early years, the congregation did not have a rabbi. Occasionally, traveling rabbis addressed the congregation.

EARNING A LIVING The Jews of colonial Newport earned their living by supplying other merchants with goods that they imported from Europe. They owned large fleets of ships that regularly sailed the established trade routes. Some of these merchant shippers became very wealthy. Men like Jacob Rivera, Aaron Lopez, and Naphtaly Hart had fine houses and many servants.

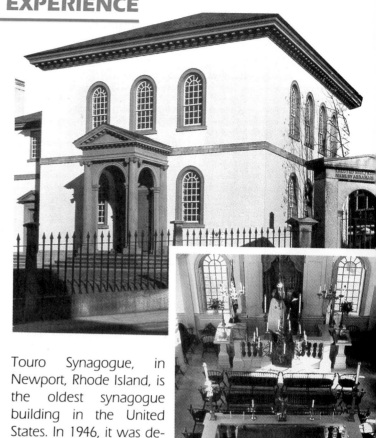

Touro Synagogue, in Newport, Rhode Island, is the oldest synagogue building in the United States. In 1946, it was declared a "national historic site."

THE AMERICAN REVOLUTION In 1776, Newport was in British hands. Many Jews who were patriots left Newport at this time rather than live under British rule.

At the end of the war, the Jews returned to their homes. But Newport was no longer the busy port that it had been. Many of its buildings had been destroyed in the war. New York and Philadelphia continued to grow, while Newport declined as a shipping and business center. Because the younger generation felt that fortunes were to be made elsewhere, many of them moved away from Newport.

Journey to Freedom

You are about to read an exciting adventure story. It is the story of how Aaron Lopez, a leading citizen of Newport, Rhode Island, rescued his brother from certain death.

Born in Portugal, Aaron Lopez had been given the Christian name Duarte. In the year 1752, when he was twenty-one, he and his wife Anne fled from Portugal to escape the Inquisition and settled in Newport, Rhode Island. As soon as they arrived in Newport, they openly declared themselves to be Jews. Duarte changed his name to Aaron; Anne became Abigail.

Aaron was a merchant shipper. He owned thirty ships and engaged in a variety of businesses. He shipped his goods to various ports in Europe, Africa, the West Indies, and the colonies. He bought molasses and made rum in his distillaries in Newport. He invented a long-burning candle made from whale fat that was very popular in England. He also bought and sold Jewish articles, such as mezuzot and prayer books.

After Abigail died in 1762, Aaron had to care for their seven children. His marriage to Sarah Rodriguez produced eight more children. Sarah was the daughter of Jacob Rodriguez Rivera, another Newport merchant.

Aaron was a respected member of the Newport Jewish community. He was president of the synagogue for many years. During the American Revolution, when the British occupied Newport, Aaron and his family fled to Leicester, Massachusetts. He died in a drowning accident when he was fifty-one.

Joseph Lopez raced up the steep staircase of his house and headed straight for his father's study.

"Father," he called breathlessly, bursting into the small room lined with maps and nautical charts. "Father, one of your ships has just dropped anchor in the harbor. Grandfather is already in his carriage on the way to the wharf to meet her. Please, Father, may I ride down with you?"

Aaron Lopez, who had been studying his nautical charts, turned and joyfully embraced his eleven-year-old son as he registered the happy news.

"Heaven be praised," he cried. "They have arrived safely. Come, Joseph. God willing, you will meet my half brother Miguel and your cousins. My ship came from Lisbon, and if our plan worked, they will be aboard."

Joseph and his father were soon in their carriage, clattering along the narrow, cobblestoned streets of the town.

Before long, Aaron and Joseph arrived at the wharf. Grandfather and a crowd of townspeople were gathered at the ramp of the ship as the captain and a dozen passengers descended.

Captain Jeremiah Osborne spotted Aaron. Smiling, he made his way toward him, followed by several passengers.

"Master Lopez," the captain boomed,

"may I present your half brother, Miguel, his wife, Joana, and their three sons. Heaven be praised, we were able to rescue them."

"Heaven will reward you my good captain." Turning to the group of passengers behind the captain, Aaron extended his arms. *"Beruchim habaim,"* he said.

Joseph was filled with questions. "Please, Father, tell me how Captain Osborne managed to get them on our ship. Are they Jewish like we are? Where did they live?"

"Be patient, Joseph. Our guests are weary from their long journey. Later, after they have rested, we will answer all of your questions."

That evening, amid the glow of candles made from whale oil, the large family sat down for dinner. "Before we hear your story," Aaron said to his brother, "I must fill in some of the background for Joseph and the other children." Aaron turned to his children and explained, "I came to Newport fifteen years ago from Portugal. There, we were secret Jews. As soon as I arrived here, I declared openly that I was a Jew."

"We know this, Father," Joseph said, "but tell us about Uncle Miguel. Why didn't he escape when you did?"

"It was difficult to escape. And for a time, life had become a little easier for the Jews. But now the Inquisition has once again begun spying upon those it regards with suspicion. In fact, people are being persecuted and executed once more."

"Were Uncle Miguel and his family in danger?"

"Yes," replied Aaron, "my agents had informed me that your uncle's life was in danger. It seemed that a servant must have told the Inquisition that the family fasted on Yom Kippur. The Inquisition warned Miguel that if the accusation was true, the family would be in grave trouble. It was just a matter of time."

"How did they manage to escape on our ship?" Joseph asked.

"I knew that I had to have a bold plan. So I sent Captain Osborne to Lisbon, the capital of Portugal, on business."

"Now I will finish the story," smiled Miguel. "You might say that Captain Osborne not only did business, he also did some tricky business. One night, there was a knock on our door. Of course, we were certain that it was the Inquisition. Who else would wake people in the middle of the night? Thank God, it was not the Inquisition but a stranger, who whispered that he was the captain of one of my brother's vessels. He produced papers with your signature and the seal of Rhode Island, Aaron, so I knew that I could trust him. He told us to dress quickly and to follow him to the pier, which we did. As soon as we boarded the ship, he lifted the anchor, and in the dead of night, we made our way out of the harbor."

"And not a day too soon," murmured Aaron. "Your lives were in danger. But now you no longer have to observe Judaism se-

cretly. Tomorrow evening, Shabbat begins. We have our own synagogue here in Newport, just four years old. The best architect in the colonies, Peter Harrison, designed it. People praise it as an excellent example of colonial architecture. When you see the interior, you will recognize it as a fine example of our Sephardic heritage as well."

On Shabbat, the Lopez family gathered with other members of the community in the beautiful synagogue. The *bimah* was in the center of the room, and the men sat on benches around it. The service was chanted in the Sephardic tradition, beneath the glow of a magnificent chandelier that had been brought from Portugal. A special prayer of *gomel* was recited, thanking God for delivering the newcomers from danger.

In the balcony, above, Joana whispered to Sarah, "Do I see a door in the floor of the *bimah*?"

"You have good eyes, Joana," Sarah replied, "Yes, it is a door. When the synagogue was designed, some of the elders who still remembered the frightening roundups by the Inquisition demanded that we have a secret passageway by which we could escape if such a raid were to occur here. But many among us felt that in the New World we are free and safe. Therefore, beneath the door there is only a ladder leading to the cellar, not a passageway for escape."

As the family walked slowly home to eat the Shabbat meal, Miguel seemed quite sad.

"Dear brother," Aaron said, "what makes you so quiet? Are you tired from your long journey?"

"No, Aaron, it is not that. I am troubled by two things far more serious. I risked my life and the lives of my family so that we could live as Jews. But now that we are safe, I must confess that we are Jews in name only, because my sons and I have not been circumcised. As you know, circumcision would have given us away. I also want my family to have Hebrew names."

"Do not worry, Miguel," Aaron replied. "You mustn't forget that many of us who were Marranos came here uncircumcised. We can correct that. When my son Joseph was born, the *mohel* performed a double circumcision—one for me and one for my son. I do recall that you were secretly named Abraham at birth. Joana, what do you wish to be called?"

"I would like to be known as Abigail," Joana replied.

"Then you will be called Abraham and Abigail from this time forward," Aaron replied.

Abraham brightened up. "Let us inform the *mohel* immediately that my three sons and I wish to be formally initiated into the faith of our ancestors. No longer will we live in fear and hide our true identity as Jews."

"Not so fast," Aaron chuckled. "There is a *mohel*, but he resides in New York. We must first write to him and make arrangements for his journey. It will be some time before he arrives, but in due course, you and my nephews will be circumcised according to the faith of our people."

The *Kiddush* that was recited in the home of Aaron Lopez that Shabbat evening was very special. A long, frightening journey had ended, and each person around the table held fast the dream of a new beginning.

Research the answers to the following questions.

1. What kind of freedom did the colony of Newport offer its citizens?

_____

2. Describe how many of the Jews of Newport earned their living.

_____

_____

3. After the American Revolution, which two American cities became major shipping centers while Newport declined in importance?

_____

4. List four facts about the synagogue in Newport, Rhode Island.

_____

_____

_____

_____

5. Make a list of all the people mentioned in this chapter who were members of the Lopez family. Create a Lopez family tree.

LOPEZ FAMILY

DISCUSSION

1. Aaron Lopez was a busy man. Yet he found time to serve his community as president of the synagogue. Discuss some busy people you know who are involved in service to your community.

2. Have you ever been to a *berit milah* or a *berit chayim*? Discuss what happens. Ask your teacher or your rabbi about the laws and customs of a *berit milah* or a *berit chayim*.

ACTIVITIES

1. Write the story of Abraham Lopez's rescue from Abraham's point of view. Why was the Inquisition watching him? How did the family manage to get on board ship without being seen? Was there any danger involved?

2. Peter Harrison designed the Touro Synagogue. There are many different and beautiful synagogue designs. Choose one of the suggestions from the list below and draw your own design for it.

- The exterior of a new synagogue
- The sanctuary of a new synagogue
- The *parochet* for the *Aron Hakodesh*
- The mantle of a Torah scroll

Design for_____

(name of synagogue)

Signing of the Constitution by Howard Chandler Christy.

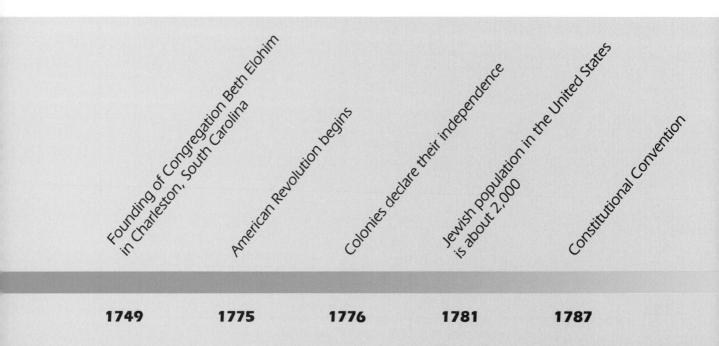

Founding of Congregation Beth Elohim in Charleston, South Carolina — **1749**

American Revolution begins — **1775**

Colonies declare their independence — **1776**

Jewish population in the United States is about 2,000 — **1781**

Constitutional Convention — **1787**

THE STRUGGLE FOR INDEPENDENCE

The American Revolution, the war in which the United States gained its independence from Great Britain, is one of the turning points of history.

By the 1750s there were settlers whose grandparents had been born in America. They did not feel loyal to a country and a king that they had never seen. People did not think that the English were fair in their dealings with them. The British government would not listen to the Americans who were asking for a chance to govern themselves. The colonists soon realized that they had to declare themselves independent and, if need be, go to war to fight for their freedom.

In this unit, you will learn that Jews contributed to the American cause. You will study how Jews fought to insure that the United States Constitution guarantees equal civic and religious rights to all people. You will also read about Jews who contributed to the development of the United States of America.

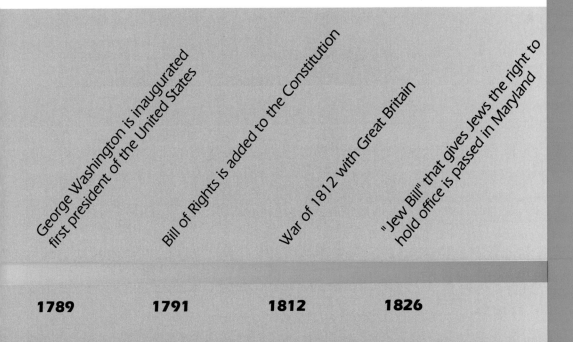

George Washington is inaugurated first president of the United States

Bill of Rights is added to the Constitution

War of 1812 with Great Britain

"Jew Bill" that gives Jews the right to hold office is passed in Maryland

1789   **1791**   **1812**   **1826**

THE AMERICAN REVOLUTION

LINKS IN HISTORY
The War for Independence

In the 1700s, more and more people began to immigrate to North America from England and other European countries. Soon there were thirteen colonies under British rule: the New England, Middle Atlantic, and Southern colonies.

By 1775, the people of the colonies no longer wanted to be British subjects. They were angry because the English king had imposed heavy taxes on the colonies. The colonists were not allowed to have representatives in the English Parliament. The English government also tried to force the colonists to trade only with Great Britain.

The colonists prepared for war. They had to make a choice. Those who wanted to be free of England were called **patriots**. Those who were loyal to England were called **loyalists**. Whatever position people took was dangerous. The patriots knew that if the colonies lost the war, England would punish them for being traitors. The loyalists knew that if the colonies won the war, they would have to leave their homes and businesses and return to England or flee to British-controlled Canada.

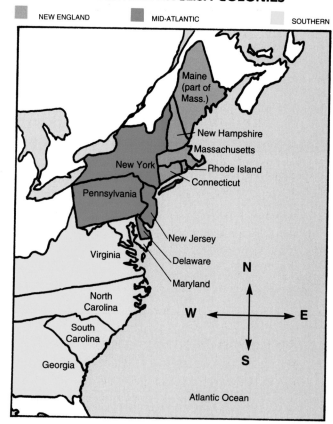

THE THIRTEEN ENGLISH COLONIES

NEW ENGLAND   MID-ATLANTIC   SOUTHERN

Maine (part of Mass.)
New Hampshire
Massachusetts
New York
Rhode Island
Connecticut
Pennsylvania
New Jersey
Virginia
Delaware
Maryland
North Carolina
South Carolina
Georgia

N
W — E
S

Atlantic Ocean

Charleston harbor in 1715. Many colonial Jews were merchants involved in the shipping trade.

THE JEWISH EXPERIENCE

In 1775, there were about two thousand Jews in the colonies. Most of them lived in New York, Philadelphia, Newport, Savannah, and Charleston. Many of them were of Sephardic origin, but the majority were now Ashkenazim from England, Holland, Germany, Poland, and Hungary.

REVOLUTION When the American Revolution began in 1775, most of the Jews in the colonies were patriots. However, the choice was not an easy one to make. Like the rest of the population, many Jews had family and business ties with Great Britain. Those who chose to be loyalists remained in British-held towns. Those who chose the side of the patriots moved their families away from British-controlled areas to places in which they could help the struggling nation. Many Jews fought as patriots during the American Revolution.

EARNING A LIVING As you have read, many colonial Jews made their living trading with England and the West Indies. The British sent them manufactured goods, while they supplied the mother country with much-needed raw materials. Fellow Jews in England often sent the Jews in the colonies a variety of items on trust. British Jews did not expect to be paid for the goods until after the merchandise was sold.

Congregation Beth Elohim, in Charleston, South Carolina, was founded in 1749.

Congregation Mikveh Israel, in Philadelphia, Pennsylvania, may have been founded as early as the 1740s.

During the American Revolution, merchant shippers had a hard time. English ships blockaded the Atlantic coast of North America. England did not allow ships carrying commercial goods for the new nation to dock at her ports. Some of the Jews in the colonies peddled goods to farmers or set up small shops in towns. In the Southern colonies, Jews traded cash crops like tobacco, indigo, and rice. They worked long hours. The hard work paid off for many of them because the population of the colonies was expanding and all kinds of items were in demand. Some Jews were **sutlers**. They supplied local militia and army units with needed goods.

EDUCATION Private groups were in charge of education. It would be many years before there was public education. The synagogues in each community organized their own schools. General and religious subjects were taught. Although Spanish was the language of many Sephardic Jews, English became the language of instruction.

The curriculum of the Jewish schools was like that of Jewish day schools today. However, in those days it was difficult to find Hebrew teachers. Teachers and rabbis were reluctant to come to the colonies. Perhaps they felt that there was *venig Yiddishkeit*, "too little Jewishness," as one pioneer wrote in a letter to the old country.

SYNAGOGUES You have already read about two synagogues that were important in colonial America—Congregation Shearith Israel in New York City and the Touro Synagogue in Newport, Rhode Island. Two other synagogues became important during the American Revolution—Congregation Mikveh Israel in Philadelphia and Congregation Beth Elohim in Charleston, South Carolina.

The Patriot "Rabbi"

During the American Revolution, many people had to find new homes. Patriots did not want to remain in towns occupied by the British. Jews who were patriots during the war years wanted to move to communities that already had a synagogue. Philadelphia was one such community. Many Jews went there and joined the synagogue, Congregation Mikveh Israel.

This story is about Gershom Mendes Seixas, the first American-born Jewish leader. Seixas came from a Sephardic family. He was not an ordained rabbi. America did not yet have ordained rabbis. Gershom Seixas was an educated Jew, a teacher, and the leader of Congregation Shearith Israel in New York. His title was chazan. *In the following story, you will read about the choices that Gershom Seixas and his fellow New York Jews made during the American Revolution.*

Gershom Mendes Seixas, the first American-born Jewish leader.

"Good people, please be quiet," Chazan Seixas begged his congregation. "The service cannot continue with this noise." Gershom Mendes Seixas, the *chazan* of Congregation Shearith Israel in New York, surveyed the congregation and wondered why the congregants had suddenly interrupted the prayer service.

Jonas Phillips, an officer of the congregation, approached the *bimah*. "Chazan," he said apologetically but loud enough for all to hear, "my boy Naphtali has just come in. He says that the British have landed on Long Island and that General Washington and his troops are retreating to Manhattan. We must stop the services and return to our homes. There may soon be fighting in the streets."

The congregants all began talking at once. Chazan Seixas raised his hands and asked for quiet once again. This time, the congregation obeyed. They looked at their leader, wondering what he would say.

"My dear friends," he began, "we will each have to make a great decision. On which side does our future lie?"

"But Chazan," a voice called out from the congregation, "how can we make such a choice? The lives and fortunes of our families are at stake."

"Let your conscience be your guide," Gershom Seixas continued. "I have already made my decision. As soon as the Sabbath is over, my family and I will leave the city. I cannot live under British rule. I decided long ago that I would support only those men and women who are loyal to the Revolutionary cause. Who wishes to leave with me?"

From all around the room came shouts of "We will go with you." However, it was not unanimous. One member stood up and said, "Chazan, I cannot leave New York. My business depends on trade with the British. If I leave and the colonists lose, we will all be punished by His Majesty, the king of Great Britain, when the war is over."

Other voices were heard: "We cannot live under tyranny." "Liberty will prevail." "We will not lose the war."

Chazan Seixas again asked for quiet. "First of all, we must finish our prayers. Then, we will all go home for the Sabbath rest. After dark, the people who wish to leave will meet here in the synagogue."

By nightfall, a majority of the members had decided to follow their leader and to flee the city. They gathered in the synagogue that evening and spoke about their plans in hushed tones. Chazan Seixas outlined the choices.

"We will leave tomorrow," he said. "We can travel in one of two directions. I plan to take my family north to Stratford, Connecticut, which is in patriot hands. The other road you may choose leads to Philadelphia."

"Chazan," Jonas Phillips said, "we have family in Philadelphia. The Jewish community there is quite large. I plan to go there. But let us leave one another with the promise that after the war is over, we shall all return to New York and rebuild our congregation."

Gershom Mendes Seixas flees British-occupied New York City.

Chazan Seixas nodded. "I pray that may be so. But in the meantime, we will need to take a few of the synagogue's holy objects. Let us borrow some of the Torah scrolls, prayer books, and silver kiddush cups. It will be impossible to get these items from Europe during wartime."

The assembled members parted with heavy hearts. However, they were comforted by the knowledge that those who were staying would keep the synagogue open for services.

A few years after the American Revolution ended, Chazan Seixas returned to Congregation Shearith Israel in New York. In 1789, Gershom Seixas attended George Washington's inauguration.

The inauguration took place in New York City. Bells were ringing, flags were waving, and guns were fired. Chazan Seixas remembered his flight from the British many years before. He thought, "It has indeed been a long journey." His lips moved as he whispered the Shehecheyanu: "Blessed is Adonai *our God, Ruler of the universe, who has granted us life and sustenance and enabled us to reach this season."*

Haym Salomon

When you think of a war hero, do you picture a brave soldier who fought for his country? Most people do. But a person does not have to be a soldier to be a war hero. As you will see, a war hero can be a person who helps his or her country in other ways.

Haym Salomon was a hero of the American Revolution. This statue of Robert Morris, President George Washington, and Salomon stands in Chicago.

Haym Salomon was born in Lissa, Poland, in about the year 1740. Because his family was not well-off, Haym left home with hopes of bettering himself. First, he wandered through several European countries. He learned many languages and gained experience in business.

Around 1773, Haym went to New York. When he arrived, he found that the colonists were planning a revolution. Haym immediately joined the Sons of Liberty, a patriot group.

When the Revolution began and the British occupied New York, Haym was arrested because of his patriot activities. One night, he escaped and fled to Philadelphia. His knowledge of business and languages helped him to establish a brokerage shop on Front Street. He was soon able to send for his wife, Rachel, and his son, Ezekial, whom he had left in New York. The family joined Congregation Mikveh Israel.

From Philadelphia, Haym supported the new American government. He helped supply the army with food and equipment. When Robert Morris became the new country's superintendent of finance, he asked Haym Salomon to assist him. At that time, the United States often could not afford to pay salaries to its representatives in the Continental Congress. Haym was asked to raise money for these salaries. He also lent money to people in need.

When the war was over, Haym returned to New York, where he bought a house on Wall Street and worked as a banker and merchant. After an illness, he died on January 6, 1785, at the age of forty-five. One account says that he died a poor man.

41

Francis Salvador

Francis Salvador was born into a Sephardic family whose members had been Conversos until they immigrated to England in the early years of the eighteenth century. His uncle Joseph had become a wealthy man in England, having bought many acres of land in South Carolina. He sold most of this land to Francis, who was determined to cultivate it.

Francis immigrated to the colony of South Carolina in 1773. He used the land that his uncle had sold him to establish a plantation. On the plantation, he grew indigo, a major cash crop in those days.

Francis Salvador loved his new home. He became active in politics and was elected to the First Provincial Congress in 1775. When South Carolina rebelled against England, together with the other colonies, Francis became a delegate to the state's General Assembly.

Salvador gave his life for the American cause. He rode out to warn his fellow farmers that Native Americans, fighting for the British, were burning plantations. During his ride, he encountered the Native American party and was killed in an ambush.

In Charleston, South Carolina, a plaque hangs in City Hall Park. It is dedicated to the memory of the famous hero and citizen of the American Revolution, Francis Salvador. It reads:

Born an aristocrat, he became
a democrat,
An Englishman, he cast his lot
with America;
True to his ancient faith, he gave
his life
For new hopes of human liberty
and understanding.

WORD BANK

Below is a list of famous people and synagogues associated with the American Revolution. Use the list to fill in the blank next to each statement.

Francis Salvador   Gershom Mendes Seixas   Robert Morris
Jonas Phillips   Congregation Shearith Israel   Haym Salomon
Congregation Beth Elohim Congregation Mikveh Israel

1. The name of the first Jewish congregation in Philadelphia, Pennsylvania.

_____

2. The Jewish congregation in New York City during the American Revolution.

_____

3. An officer of Congregation Shearith Israel who fled to Philadelphia during the American Revolution. _____

4. A Jewish hero from South Carolina who was killed when he rode out to warn his fellow farmers about Native Americans who were fighting for the British.

_____

5. The American superintendent of finance during the American Revolution.

_____

6. The *chazan* of Congregation Shearith Israel and Congregation Mikveh Israel.

_____

7. A Polish-born Jew who aided the American cause by raising money.

_____

8. The first Jewish congregation in Charleston, South Carolina.

_____

DISCUSSION

1. Gershom Mendes Seixas was a strong Jewish leader. Discuss the qualities that a leader must have. What made Seixas a leader?

2. Haym Salomon was not a soldier, but he was a courageous man. Give some examples of his courage. Do you have a story about someone you know who is courageous?

ACTIVITIES

1. Make a list of reasons for being a patriot and another for being a loyalist. One reason for each choice appears below.

Patriot

a. Born in America

b. _____

c. _____

d. _____

Loyalist

a. Close family lives in England

b. _____

c. _____

d. _____

2. Choose one of the people listed in the **Word Bank** on page 43. Design a monument and write a dedication on its base to the person that you chose.

RELIGIOUS FREEDOM FOR ALL AMERICANS

LINKS IN HISTORY

Writing the Constitution

The American Revolution was over. The United States was now a country made up of thirteen states. The colonists had to decide what kind of government they wanted. They knew that they did not want to be governed by a king. They wanted their lawmakers to represent the people. In May 1787, the Constitutional Convention began, with George Washington presiding. The Constitution was adopted on March 4, 1789.

The writers of the Constitution tried to think of every situation that might arise in their new country. But they knew that events they could not predict would also occur. Therefore, in Article V, they included ways to amend the Constitution.

In 1791, the first ten amendments were added to the Constitution. They are called the **Bill of Rights**. These amendments protect the freedoms of the American people. The First Amendment proclaims our four basic rights: freedom of religion, freedom of speech, freedom of the press, and freedom to assemble peaceably.

THE JEWISH EXPERIENCE

Most of the two thousand Jews who lived in the United States in 1781 were patriots. They had worked and fought for America's freedom. Now they looked forward to living in the new republic.

JEWS AND THE CONSTITUTION In 1787, American Jews were anxiously awaiting the outcome of the Constitutional Convention that was meeting in Philadelphia. They hoped that the Constitution would give equal rights to all citizens. No one was more concerned than Jonas Phillips, a Philadelphia businessman and a member of Congregation Mikveh Israel. He wrote to the delegates, asking them to insure that government officials should not have to take a religious oath of any kind.

Jonas Phillips.

Since the discussions of the Constitutional Convention were secret, Jonas Phillips found out only later that the delegates had already written Article VI of the Constitution, which states that no one elected or appointed to a federal position has to take a religious oath.

Jonas Phillips and all American Jews were even more delighted when they later read the First Amendment to the Constitution, contained in the Bill of Rights. It says: "Congress shall make no law respecting an establishment of religion, or prohibiting the free exercise thereof; . . ."

After the Constitution was accepted by the individual states, there was much rejoicing. In Philadelphia, a great parade with many floats was held. The streets were decorated, and children were given a day off from school. Newspapers recorded that a "rabbi of the Jews" marched arm in arm with Christian ministers. When the parade ended, there was an outdoor banquet. The

newspapers also recorded another amazing sight—a table filled with kosher food. On the table were "salmon, bread and crackers, almonds, and raisins." Toasts were offered to General George Washington and the new Constitution.

BUILDING A COMMUNITY During the years in which the Constitution was written and adopted, the Jews in America were struggling to create a community. Jews organized their lives around their synagogues. The majority of the synagogues followed the Sephardic ritual. The first Ashkenazic synagogue, Bnai Jeshurun Congregation in New York City, was not formed until 1825.

People found pleasure in being Jewish, although many of them were not particularly religious. They were concerned with the problems of their fellow Jews in other countries and tried to help them. They wanted the best education for their children, but there were few good Hebrew teachers. Since the Jewish community was still small, there were not enough eligible marriage partners. As a result, intermarriage was quite common.

Jews were excited about the freedoms that the Constitution provided. At last, they had the opportunity to be citizens of a country that did not discriminate against them because they were Jewish. All areas of life were now opened to them. They could be doctors, army and naval officers, writers, businesspeople, artists, and dreamers. But sometimes they discovered to their dismay that the freedoms that were written on paper did not exist in reality. Jews found that they had to fight against prejudice in order to preserve those rights promised them in the Constitution.

IN THEIR OWN WORDS

A Letter from President Washington

When George Washington became the first president of the United States, many people wrote letters of congratulations to him. One of the letters came from members of the Touro Synagogue in Newport, Rhode Island. George Washington answered the letter. Here is an excerpt from his answer. In part of the letter, he used a quotation from the Bible. It is from the prophet Micah (4:4). Can you find it in the Bible?

> . . . for happily, the government of the United States, which gives to bigotry no sanction, to persecution no assistance, requires only that they who live under its protection should demean themselves as good citizens. . . . May the children of . . . Abraham who dwell in this land continue to merit and enjoy the good will of the other inhabitants, while everyone shall sit in safety under his own vine and fig-tree, and there shall be none to make him afraid.

fervent wishes for my felicity. May the children of the Stock of Abraham, who dwell in this land, continue to merit and enjoy the good will of the other Inhabitants, while every one shall sit in safety under his own vine and figtree, and there shall be none to make him afraid. May the father of all mercies scatter light and not darkness in our paths, and make us all in our several vocations useful here, and in his own due time and way everlastingly happy.

G Washington

The "Jew Bill"

The Constitution guarantees all Americans civil and religious liberties. When this document was written, however, some state constitutions still contained many biased laws. In some states, a person who was elected or appointed to a state office had to swear that he believed in Christianity.

The story below tells how two men, one a Scot and the other a Jew, fought for the civil rights of all the citizens of Maryland.

"My good friend, it is a pleasure to see you again," Solomon Etting said, as he rose from his chair to greet Thomas Kennedy, a delegate to the Maryland legislature. "Thank you for coming."

"I came as quickly as I could," Kennedy replied. "When my friend Solomon Etting sends me a message to call on him, I know that it must be urgent. Your grave face tells me that you are troubled."

"Yes, I'm afraid that I am troubled," Solomon said, shifting restlessly. "The Jews of Baltimore are grateful to you for the work you have done on our behalf. Twice you have introduced a bill in the Maryland legislature to eliminate the religious oath. And twice the legislature has defeated your bill."

"To put it bluntly, Thomas," Solomon continued, "why must the newspapers refer to your bill as the 'Jew Bill'? Can we do anything about this? It is incredible that the state of Maryland still maintains that only a Christian can hold a state office, despite the fact that our Constitution guarantees all our citizens freedom of religion. We are not just talking about the rights of Jews but about the rights of all people."

"I agree with you, my friend," Kennedy nodded. "Indeed, the term 'Jew Bill'

SKETCH

OF

PROCEEDINGS IN THE

Legislature of Maryland,

DECEMBER SESSION, 1818,

ON WHAT IS COMMONLY CALLED

The Jew Bill;

CONTAINING

THE REPORT OF THE COMMITTEE

APPOINTED BY THE HOUSE OF DELEGATES

"To consider the justice and expediency of extending to those persons professing the Jewish Religion, the same privileges that are enjoyed by Christians:"

TOGETHER WITH

The Bill reported by the Committee,

AND

THE SPEECHES

OF

THOMAS KENNEDY, Esq. OF WASHINGTON COUNTY,

AND

H. M. BRACKENRIDGE, Esq. OF BALTIMORE CITY.

Baltimore:

PRINTED BY JOSEPH ROBINSON,

Circulating Library, corner of Market and Belvidere-streets.

1819.

The "Jew Bill," which granted the Jews of Maryland equal political rights, was ratified in 1826.

does sound one-sided. We must rewrite the law to give all people the chance to hold office. It is unfortunate that our state has many uneducated people. They are convinced that a state official who is not Christian would harm America. It is an old prejudice. I fear that their chief concern is maintaining their own power.

"But the press is on our side," Kennedy continued. "I plan to reintroduce a bill that would do away with the religious oath once and for all. The press is doing us a favor by keeping the issue alive."

"How can I help you?" Solomon asked. "Just recently, my son came to me and said that he wishes to attend the University of Pennsylvania to study law. His request brought tears to my eyes."

"I don't quite understand," Thomas interrupted, "why that request brought you such anguish."

"You forget, my friend, that the practice of law in Maryland is a state office. Such an office requires the religious oath. If my son wishes to pursue his desire to practice law, he will have to leave Maryland and live in another state, where he would not have to take a religious oath. We are a very close family. It would pain me deeply if he would have to live apart from us."

"Thank you, Solomon," Kennedy said.

"Why do you thank me? I have only poured out my troubles to you," Solomon replied.

"I thank you because you have given me added courage to introduce my bill once again. This time, we will not lose. If just one person in our state is not free to participate fully in government, then none of us is free."

"I will help you, Thomas. My friends and I will write a petition to the state legislature, arguing for our right to hold office. This issue is not only a Jewish problem. It threatens the rights of every citizen in our free country."

"The legislature meets in two weeks," Thomas said. "Let's hope that we will be successful."

"Hear ye, hear ye! The legislature of the state of Maryland is now in session. Will the delegates please take their seats."

"Mister Speaker," Thomas Kennedy said, rising from his seat, "I have before me a petition signed by three citizens of our great state, Jacob Cohen, Solomon Etting, and Levi Solomon. I request permission for my friend and an outstanding citizen of Baltimore, Colonel William Worthington, to read the petition and speak on behalf of my bill."

"You have our permission," the speaker of the house replied. "Read the petition."

Colonel Worthington walked to the speaker's stand and began. "The petitioners protest the fact that they have been disqualified from political office because of the religious oath required by the constitution of the state of Maryland. They ask that they be given the same civil rights that they enjoy under the Constitution of the United States. They hope that this session of the legislature will grant them these rights.

"Therefore," Worthington continued, "I once again request that this legislature pass a law that does away with the religious oath. I remind you that under the United States Constitution, a Jew can become president of the United States. Yet here in Maryland, he cannot hold even the lowliest public office."

"But the Jews are the enemies of Christianity," a voice called out.

"If we pass such a law, they will try to make us all Jews," another voice cried.

"Gentlemen," John Tyson, another delegate, spoke above the noise, "we don't have the right to speak out against another religion just because it is different from our own! To do so lessens all of us. The Jews have suffered greatly from persecution over the ages. Is it not time that the biased part of our state constitution be abolished? Thomas Kennedy has fought a long, hard battle for equal rights. I say that the Jews and all people should have the same rights in Maryland that the Constitution of the United States gives them. I move that Mr. Kennedy's bill be passed."

"Who favors Mr. Kennedy's bill? Let him show his agreement by a display of hands," the house speaker called out.

"Sir," the house clerk reported to the speaker after the count, "the bill is passed, 45 to 32."

In the following year, on January 6, 1826, the *Baltimore Register* announced that the bill had been confirmed. The newspaper's headline read: "Jews are free. A disgraceful part of our constitution has been changed."

Now it was Solomon Etting's turn to pay a call on Thomas Kennedy. "Thomas," he said, "you have performed a great service for our state and our country. My people thank you. Soon I am going to test the new law."

"How do you plan to do that?" Thomas asked.

"I shall run for the Baltimore city council in this year's election."

"Solomon," Thomas replied, "you have earned the respect of the people of this city. I have no doubt that you will win."

Judah Touro

Judah Touro.

Judah Touro was born in 1775, on the eve of the American Revolution. His father, Isaac Touro, was the *chazan* of the synagogue in Newport, Rhode Island.

In 1802, when Judah was twenty-six years old, he settled in the Spanish-French town of New Orleans. At that time, New Orleans was a small town of ten thousand people, located at the mouth of the Mississippi River. There, Judah opened a shop and sold goods that he imported from his native New England. The next year, Thomas Jefferson purchased the Louisiana Territory from France, and New Orleans became a part of the United States.

Judah's business grew. He purchased property. He bought and sold goods of every kind. He shipped some of these goods to Europe. Others were sent north up the Mississippi River to small settlements.

Toward the end of his life, Judah Touro became an observant Jew. He closed his offices on Shabbat and was often seen praying in the synagogue on that day. He used his wealth to support various charities. A kindly man, he helped individuals who needed assistance. He never asked to be honored for the *tzedakah* he gave, nor did he want to be thanked.

About two weeks before his death in 1854, he drew up his final will. Since Judah had never married, he directed that a large portion of his money—almost $500,000— be distributed among various organizations. Judah gave a gift to almost every synagogue in the United States. His gifts enabled his own synagogue in New Orleans and a church in that city to erect new buildings. In addition, Judah's money built the New Orleans Public Library, one of the first in the country, and established a hospital in New Orleans.

Judah also gave $60,000 to Sir Moses Montefiore, an important British Jew, to help him build the first Jewish neighborhood outside the walls of the old city of Jerusalem. That neighborhood is called Yemin Moshe. In addition, Judah contributed funds to the Jews Hospital Society in New York. This hospital is today called Mount Sinai.

Judah Touro wished to be buried in the old cemetery near the synagogue in Newport, Rhode Island. The following epitaph appears on his tombstone: "The last of his name, he inscribed it in the Book of Philanthropy, to be remembered forever."

51

NAME BANK

Use the **Name Bank** below to answer the following questions.

Jonas Phillips   Judah Touro   Thomas Kennedy   Solomon Etting

1. He wrote a law that eliminated the religious oath from the Maryland constitution._____

2. He wrote a letter to the Constitutional Convention, asking the delegates not to include a religious test for taking the oath of office._____

3. This Jewish businessman worked with Thomas Kennedy to abolish the religious oath from the Maryland constitution._____

4. In his will, he left his entire fortune to various organizations._____

DISCUSSION

1. Religious freedom is an important American civil right. A current topic of debate is whether or not there should be prayer in our public schools. Some people believe that a moment of silent prayer is important and is a good way to begin the school day. Others believe that school prayer is against the principle that church and state should be separate. What do you think?

2. If you had the opportunity to give half a million dollars to different charities, which ones would you choose? Select four charities and discuss your reasons for choosing these charities.

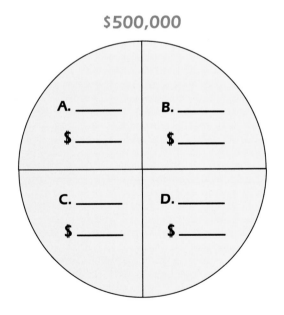

$500,000

A. _____   B. _____
$ _____ $ _____

C. _____   D. _____
$ _____ $ _____

List the charities and your reasons for giving *tzedakah* to each one.

A. _____

_____

B. _____

_____

C. _____

_____

D. _____

_____

3. At the banquet that took place in Philadelphia to celebrate the acceptance of the Constitution, one table was filled with kosher food. Discuss why kosher food was made available at this event.

ACTIVITIES

1. As a class, create a wall chart that shows how your Jewish community is organized. Draw pictures or take photos to illustrate the following:

- Synagogues: Names, leaders, various programs
- Jewish community center: Name, executive director's name, programs in session
- Educational institutions: Colleges, religious schools, day schools, special schools, museums
- Special stores and community services: Bakery, butcher, delicatessen, caterers, etc.

2. Almost every synagogue and school has been built with the help of *tzedakah*. The names of the donors are usually displayed on wall plaques. Choose a person in your community who has contributed to your synagogue or school. Interview that person, or ask your teacher or rabbi to tell you about that person's life. Make a "thank-you" booklet, consisting of all the students' written interviews.

The Huerfano Butte by Solomon Nunes Carvalho is an engraving from the 1856 book *Memoirs of My Life* by John Charles Frémont.

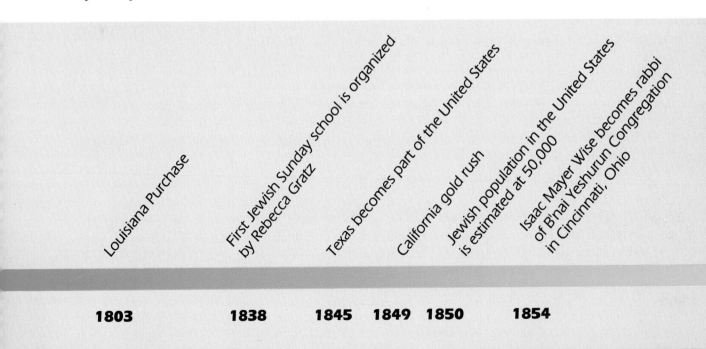

Louisiana Purchase

First Jewish Sunday school is organized by Rebecca Gratz

Texas becomes part of the United States

California gold rush

Jewish population in the United States is estimated at 50,000

Isaac Mayer Wise becomes rabbi of B'nai Yeshurun Congregation in Cincinnati, Ohio

1803　　　**1838**　　**1845**　**1849**　**1850**　　**1854**

AMERICA EXPANDS

U
N
I
T

III

By the early 1800s, American Jewish life had begun to change. Jews joined the thousands of people who were moving west in search of a better life. They struggled to make a living and to overcome prejudice. They also worked hard to keep their ties to Judaism strong.

By the mid-1800s, thousands of newcomers were immigrating to America from Europe. Many of the Jewish immigrants came from German lands. The German Jewish immigrants appreciated the new freedoms and opportunities that America offered. They began to adapt their Jewish practices to an American way of life. By 1860, the Jewish population in the United States had grown to about one hundred and twenty-five thousand. The many Jewish communities throughout the country tried to stay united.

But at the very same time that the Jews were struggling for unity, the United States was about to become a divided country. The Civil War broke out in 1861. You will read about the Jewish reaction to slavery in this period and about the young Jewish men who joined the armies of the Union and the Confederacy.

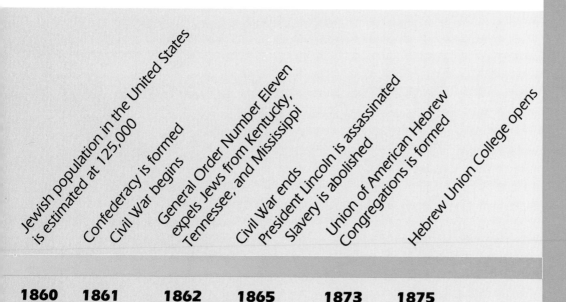

Jewish population in the United States is estimated at 125,000

Confederacy is formed

Civil War begins

General Order Number Eleven expels Jews from Kentucky, Tennessee, and Mississippi

Civil War ends

President Lincoln is assassinated

Slavery is abolished

Union of American Hebrew Congregations is formed

Hebrew Union College opens

1860   1861   1862   1865   1873   1875

C H A P T E R 6

MORE LAND—MORE PEOPLE

LINKS IN HISTORY

The Louisiana Purchase

President Thomas Jefferson added a gigantic portion of territory to the United States in 1803 when he encouraged Congress to buy land from France. This territory was called the Louisiana Purchase. It included almost the entire middle section of the United States. The new territory began at the Mississippi River and extended to the Rocky Mountains. It bordered Canada in the north and stretched as far south as New Orleans. The purchase doubled the size of the United States.

The government of the United States printed posters advertising cheap land for sale and distributed them in Europe. Many of the people living in Europe at that time were unhappy for several reasons. Wars were common, and governments were constantly changing. People were too poor to feed their families. There was religious and political persecution. Thousands of Europeans felt that they could create a new and better life for themselves and their families in the United States. They gathered what

LOUISIANA PURCHASE 1803

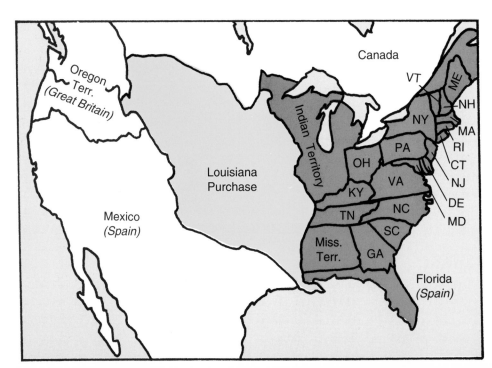

☐ LOUISIANA PURCHASE

■ UNITED STATES

belongings they possessed and bought tickets for the steamer trip across the ocean to the New World.

When many of these immigrants arrived, they made their way west. Once there, they settled on farms or in small towns. Cities like Milwaukee, Cleveland, Cincinnati, and Detroit were established during this period.

From these cities in today's Midwest, some of the immigrants made their way even farther west, toward the Pacific Ocean. In 1845, Texas declared its independence from Mexico and became part of the United States. New Mexico, Arizona, Colorado, Utah, and most of California also joined the Union.

Immigrants traveled to the West Coast by covered wagons over the Rocky Mountains or by steamer boats around the southern tip of South America. In 1849, gold was discovered in California. As thousands of people rushed west hoping to strike it rich, new cities sprung up almost overnight. In time, railroads were built to connect the newly settled areas.

THE JEWISH EXPERIENCE

The Jews who lived in Germany suffered under harsh anti-Jewish laws. German Jews longed for a land with open spaces and freedom. When German Jews heard that the United States needed settlers, many of them decided to emigrate.

Thousands of Ashkenazic Jews from Germany arrived in the United States in the years following 1830. By 1850, the Jewish population in America had grown to about fifty thousand.

FINDING WORK How did the immigrants make a living in the United States? Those who were carpenters, tailors, and watchmakers came with skills. But most of the immigrants had few skills and little money. One of the ways they could get started was to become a peddler. Now that the Louisiana Purchase had doubled the size of the United States, there were new routes to travel and many new farm areas and small towns in which to sell. It was a rough and lonely life for many German Jewish immigrants. Very often, married men left their families in Europe until they could earn enough money to pay for their loved ones' passage.

THE WEST As soon as the United States bought the Louisiana Territory, explorers began to chart the trails to the Far West. Colonel John Charles Frémont led several expeditions beyond the Rocky Mountains to the Pacific Ocean. In 1853, Colonel Frémont was accompanied by a young Sephardic Jew, Solomon Nunes Carvalho. Both a photographer and an artist, Carvalho undertook to record the journey. He also kept a written account of the hardships that the expedition encountered. When he returned east, he published his writings and art work in a book called *Incidents of Travel and Adventure in the Far West*. Solomon Nunes Carvalho's bravery helped pave the way for others who later made the difficult trip to California.

57

THE JEWISH PEDDLER

Imagine that you were the only Jewish person living within hundreds of miles. There was no synagogue, none of the special foods that you would like to have, and no family with which to celebrate holidays.

Travel to this area was difficult. The only existing roads were Indian paths. You promised the family you left behind in Germany that you would make enough money to send for them as soon as possible. When you reached Cincinnati, Ohio, a supplier gave you a pack of goods—some cloth, pots and dishes, needles, pins, and combs. He told you that you could pay him after you had sold it all. You put the pack on your back and set out across the prairie.

At first, it was very hard because you did not know much English. When you tried to explain in German to the farmer's wife why you had knocked on her door, she stared at you. But when you showed her what was inside your pack, she bought some of your wares.

When the winter's blizzards piled up snow in huge drifts, you wondered why you had ever left Germany. But when you had enough money to buy a horse and a cart, life became a little easier. You could cover more territory and take along more goods to peddle.

Spring came, and it was Passover. How you missed your family, as well as the holiday rituals—the special housecleaning, the baking of *matzot,* the seder table. All you had was a bed in a rooming house. Just at this time, however, more Jews began to arrive in town. You were kept busy explaining to them how to set up a peddler's business.

After another year or so passed, you had enough money to send for your wife and children. They arrived, wide-eyed. This was a larger land than they had imagined. "Why," your wife asked, "do you have to be on the road so much? This town is fairly big. Why don't you set up a small store from which you could sell your goods? The farmers come

to town to sell their grain. When they are here, they will buy their supplies from you."

So you set up a little store on the main street and, sure enough, the farmers and the townspeople came and bought.

In a few years, there were a dozen Jewish families in town, with more than enough men for a *minyan.* Together, you rented a hall for Rosh Hashanah. At last, you had a congregation.

In a few years, life changed swiftly. The congregation outgrew the rented hall. You were ready to build a synagogue and hire a rabbi. Your business prospered, and the size of your store grew. By the time you had grandchildren, you owned a large department store. As more and more people arrived, your little town became a city.

Canvas for Sale
The Story of Levi Strauss

Levi Strauss.

"Tents for sale. Fine, strong canvas tents for sale." Levi Strauss stood on a dusty hill overlooking San Francisco Bay. All around him were hundreds of tents and shacks, hastily put up by men who were arriving every day in search of their dreams. The year was 1853. Gold had been discovered a few years earlier in the sleepy outskirts of the village. Overnight, the population of San Francisco had soared. The gold rush was on.

"What have we here?" a grizzly-looking gold prospector wearing torn pants stopped and looked at the piles of canvas lying on the ground.

"The finest-quality canvas from the East Coast," replied Levi. "I can make a waterproof tent for you in no time at all."

"Nope," replied the prospector, "I already have a tent."

Levi Strauss looked disappointed as the prospector walked over to the next street peddler to examine his wares.

"Canvas for sale. Let me make you a fine tent," Levi called to the passing crowd. But his heart wasn't in it. Levi had just come to San Francisco from New York. His sister, Fanny, and her husband, David Stern, a dry-goods merchant, lived in San Francisco. "Bring canvas," they had written to the twenty-year-old immigrant in New York. "People are arriving here daily by the thousands. This is a boom town. People need canvas for tents."

Later that evening, as he sat with his sister and brother-in-law, he told them of his difficulty selling the canvas. "There are too many peddlers trying to sell the same thing," he said. "But tomorrow is another day. I will try again."

Early the next morning, Levi was back at his usual spot. It was a bright, sunny day, cooled by a steady breeze blowing in from the bay. The first few customers were polite. Some bought the canvas, but many were just looking.

Levi was beginning to have that discouraged feeling again when a short man with a beard approached. "You have good-quality canvas," he said, as he fingered the material.

"I have the best-quality canvas. It is waterproof and durable," Levi replied. "Perhaps you need some for a tent?"

"No, I have a tent. But do you have any pants?"

"Pants? No, all I have is this canvas," Levi answered, looking at the poorly fitting overalls that the prospector was

Levi Strauss sold canvas pants to miners during the California gold rush.

wearing. Just as the miner was about to walk away, Levi exclaimed, "Wait! I will make you a pair of pants using this canvas. I promise that they will fit well and last longer than the pants you are wearing."

"You've got yourself a deal," smiled the prospector. "Mining is tough on a man's overalls. They tear easily. If your pants will be as sturdy as you say, I'll even buy a second pair."

That night, Levi told his brother-in-law, David, about his idea. "The gold miners need pants made of strong material. Our canvas is just the thing. Let's open up a dry-goods store where we will not only sell canvas but also mining clothes made from canvas!"

David agreed. They soon opened a store near the San Francisco waterfront. They made strong, sturdy pants. The miners loved the pants because they did not wear out or tear easily. Word spread, and soon Levi and his brother-in-law were so busy that they had to move to a bigger store. By 1860, they had begun making pants from denim.

Over the years, their company became very successful. In 1873, Levi Strauss and his brother-in-law built a large factory. Near the turn of the nineteenth century, Levi decided it was time to reduce his busy schedule. David Stern had passed away many years before.

Levi asked his nephews, David Stern's four sons, to take over the company. "I know that you will continue to run our business the same way that your father and I did," he said. "I do, however, have one request."

"What is it, Uncle Levi?" Jacob Stern asked.

"Long ago, I promised that if I succeeded in America, I would give *tzedakah*. I have kept this promise. I hope that you will continue my practice."

"That will not be a problem, Uncle Levi," replied Jacob. "My brothers and I fully agree about the importance of this *mitzvah*. Is there any special way in which you want us to give *tzedakah*?"

"Yes," replied Levi, "I would like you to give at least some of the money anonymously, as I have done in the past."

"Giving *tzedakah* anonymously is the highest form of giving," the nephews replied. "We promise that in the years to come, our company will continue this practice."

Uriah Phillips Levy

Uriah Phillips Levy was born in Philadelphia, Pennsylvania, in the year 1792. He became the highest-ranking Jew in the United States Navy. He and his cousin Mordecai Manuel Noah were grandsons of Jonas Phillips, the Pennsylvania businessman whom you read about in Chapter 5.

When Uriah was ten years old, he ran away to sea. He rose from the lowly position of cabin boy to the highest rank in the United States Navy at that time—that of commodore.

Uriah greatly admired Thomas Jefferson. Like Jefferson, he believed that all Americans were entitled to live their lives with dignity. He spoke up for the freedoms stated in the First Amendment. He was proud of his Jewish heritage and fought against prejudice and injustice. Uriah bought Jefferson's home in Monticello and preserved the mansion. He also had a sculpture of Jefferson placed in the Capitol building in Washington, D.C.

But Uriah's life was not easy. At that time, if a sailor did something wrong, he was whipped. Uriah was against this type of punishment, called **corporal punishment**. Other officers did not agree with Uriah, and they brought charges against him for being too permissive. The secretary of the navy called for a hearing on these charges. The result was that Uriah's commission in the navy was taken away.

The court of inquiry met in 1857, about five years before Uriah's death. He was questioned about his abilities to command

Uriah Phillips Levy protested the use of corporal punishment in the United States Navy.

a ship and about his methods of dealing with sailors. Uriah felt the real reason that his fellow officers had brought charges against him was because he was a Jew. He defended himself. In the end, his navy commission was restored, and he was promoted to the rank of commodore.

Mordecai Manuel Noah

Are you a daydreamer? Do you sometimes close your eyes and imagine things that you would like to do and places that you would like to visit? Some people have very grand daydreams. They take their dreams seriously and try to make them come true.

One such dreamer was Mordecai Manuel Noah, a well-known American Jew who lived in the early 1800s. He was born in Philadelphia in 1785. His parents died when he was young, and he was raised by his grandparents, Jonas and Rebecca Phillips.

In 1813, Noah was appointed the American consul to Tunis, a city in North Africa. He served in that post for two years, during which time he established ties with local Jews and defended American interests. However, certain people both in Tunis and the United States were prejudiced. They felt that a Jew should not hold this job. In 1815, the government called Noah home from Tunis, and he settled in New York City.

Noah became a well-known journalist, politician, and writer. Among other things, he wrote about the difficult lives of his fellow Jews in Europe. He had seen their misery on his journeys to and from Tunis. He started to dream about creating a colony to which all persecuted Jews could go and live in peace.

His dream began to take shape. He decided to establish such a place in New York State. He selected an island near the Niagara River, New York, called Grand Island. On September 2, 1825, Noah dedicated the land and called it Ararat. Many people came to the dedication. But no one ever came to live in Ararat, even though posters advertising the community were distributed throughout Europe. Today, all that is left of Noah's dream is an engraved foundation stone.

In 1819, John Adams, second president of the United States, wrote to Mordecai Manuel Noah, expressing support for a Jewish homeland: "For I really wish the Jews again in Judea an independent nation."

CHAPTER 6 CHECKUP

Reread the chapter to find the answers to the following questions.

1. Give four reasons why Europeans wanted to come to the United States.

   a. _____

   _____

   b. _____

   _____

   c. _____

   _____

   d. _____

   _____

2. From which European country did most of the Jews who immigrated to the United States between 1830 and 1850 come? _____

3. Why did San Francisco attract immigrants like Levi Strauss? _____

   _____

4. _____ and _____ were grandsons of Jonas Phillips.

5. _____ defended himself before a congressional inquiry.

6. The photographer, writer, and artist who explored the Far West with Colonel John Charles Frémont was _____.

7. Mordecai Manuel Noah tried to create a colony for Jews on Grand Island near Niagara Falls. He named the place _____.

DISCUSSION

1. Describe some of the difficulties that an immigrant in the early 1800s encountered.

2. Imagine that you were an early Jewish immigrant living without the company of fellow Jews. Which holidays and rituals would you try to keep? On the next page, tell how you would observe Jewish holidays and rituals.

JEWISH HOLIDAYS AND RITUALS	OBSERVANCES
a. _____	a. _____
b. _____	b. _____
c. _____	c. _____
d. _____	d. _____
e. _____	e. _____

3. According to Jewish custom, the most admired way of giving *tzedakah* is to give anonymously, as Levi Strauss did. Discuss how you feel about this. Ask your teacher or rabbi if your synagogue and school has any anonymous donors.

ACTIVITIES

1. Write a letter to your family in Europe, describing your life in the United States as a Jewish immigrant in the early 1800s.

2. Write a short one-act play about ten-year-old Uriah Levy's decision to become a cabin boy. Why did he run away to sea? Did the fact that he was Jewish cause a problem for him with the other crew members?

3. Create a poster like the ones the United States government might have used to attract European immigrants.

C H A P T E R 7

JUDAISM CHANGES

LINKS IN HISTORY

Religion in America

In 1828, Andrew Jackson was elected president. American politics began to change. Jackson was the first president to represent the average citizen, especially workers and small farmers. People began to realize that they could play an active role in politics and bring about change.

Many of the changes that took place at this time came about through the efforts of religious groups. In the first half of the 1800s, there were many religious groups in the United States. These groups built thousands of churches. They also organized colleges, schools, orphanages, and other organizations to help people. Some of the groups, like the Shakers and the Mormons, founded their own communities. Churches and synagogues became important community centers.

Religious groups, along with other community organizations, worked to reform things that needed change. To **reform** means to "improve or change for the better." Many groups joined together to improve prisons, care for the sick, and pass child-labor laws.

THE JEWISH EXPERIENCE

It was not easy to practice Judaism in the frontier towns. It took years before there were enough Jewish families in some small towns to organize a synagogue. Observing the Sabbath was hard for people who earned their living as traveling peddlers. Kosher food was often impossible to obtain. There were few people in the frontier towns who could teach about Judaism. There were even fewer people who could teach the Hebrew language.

The Jewish communities in the cities also had problems. Most of the new immigrants were so busy earning a living that they did not have time to devote to a synagogue. Many of the younger Jews did not find the synagogue services appealing and had begun to neglect the Sabbath.

Moses Mendelssohn helped introduce the Enlightenment to Jews.

WINDS OF CHANGE Jewish leaders realized that Jews had to be educated in religious observances and that changes had to be made in the synagogue services. Such changes in institutional life are called reforms.

As a result, by the end of the 1840s, many reforms had been made in American Jewish congregations. Even the very traditional congregations had become more Americanized. Some prayers were read in English. Sermons were preached in English. People began to expect more quiet and order in the synagogue. People who refused to accept their congregation's changes resigned and organized new synagogues more to their liking. For the first time, many communities had more than one synagogue. Jews now could join the synagogue of their choice.

JEWISH UNITY Soon there were so many new synagogues that Jewish leaders began to fear that Jews were becoming strangers to one another. Efforts had to be made to bring order and unity to the various Jewish groups. At this time, two leaders stood out in their efforts to strengthen and unify Judaism. They were both immigrants from Europe. One was a rabbi, Isaac Mayer Wise, and the other was a *chazan* and an educator, Isaac Leeser.

EUROPEAN ORIGINS OF THE REFORM MOVEMENT During the Middle Ages, Jews had been frequently persecuted by the Christian population of Europe. They were disliked because they refused to accept Christianity. Jews were often forced to live in **ghettos**. A ghetto is a section of a city in which many members of a minority group are forced to live. Jews were also restricted in the kinds of work they could do to earn a living.

In the 1700s, a new movement swept Europe. This movement was called the **Enlightenment**. Many educated Christians began to think about life and science in new, more reasonable ways. They read more and were less afraid of people who believed differently than they did.

In Germany, a learned Jewish philosopher, Moses Mendelssohn, wrote that people should be tolerant of one another's differences. Mendelssohn also thought that the Jews living in the ghettos should try to adapt to modern times. He translated the Torah into German so that Jews could study the sacred books of the Jewish religion in the language of the land in which they lived.

JEWS BECOME CITIZENS After the French Revolution in 1789, Jews throughout much of Europe were granted citizenship. Many Jews were thrilled with their new freedom. They left the ghettos and tried to live like everyone else. Some of

The French Revolution, which began with the storming of the Bastille, granted Jews citizenship in countries throughout Europe.

these Jews stopped being observant. Others went so far as to convert to Christianity.

THE FIRST REFORMS Many Jewish leaders became very concerned about the survival of Judaism. Israel Jacobson, a German Jewish businessman, opened a school in Seesen, Germany, to educate Jewish children both in the modern sciences and the beliefs of Judaism. He held Sabbath services for the children. He taught them to sing Jewish hymns and instructed them by giving weekly sermons. Soon many parents and townspeople chose to attend his services rather than those in the local synagogue.

Encouraged by people's responses, Jacobson moved to Berlin, where he conducted the same type of services in his home. This time, however, he met with opposition.

Israel Jacobson, one of the founders of the Reform movement in Europe, made many changes in Jewish worship.

OPPOSITION The opposition came from Jews who did not want to see changes made in the services. They felt that changes would weaken Judaism and divide the Jewish people. These people complained to the government that those who attended Jacobson's services were rebels. The police were sent to stop the services.

A few years later, in 1817, another attempt to reform the services was made in Hamburg, Germany. This time, the government did not interfere. The reformers built a house of worship and called it a **temple**, borrowing the name from the ancient Temple in Jerusalem.

In time, Reform congregations were established throughout Europe. Many German Jews had begun to immigrate to the United States. Among them were young leaders of the German Reform movement, who were anxious to try out their ideas on these shores. Men like Max Lilienthal, Isaac Mayer Wise, David Einhorn, and Kaufmann Kohler were among the first rabbis to come to America.

AMERICA'S FIRST REFORM TEMPLES In 1824, a group of young people, including a well-known journalist, Isaac Harby, tried to bring changes to Congregation Beth Elohim in Charleston, South Carolina. At first, their ideas were rejected. As a result, they broke with the synagogue and formed a new group called the Reformed Society of Israelites. But in 1836, Congregation Beth Elohim invited Gustav Poznanski to be its leader. Four years later, the congregants installed an organ. As a result of these reforms, most of the members of the Reformed Society rejoined Congregation Beth Elohim.

Rabbi Kaufmann Kohler helped formulate the beliefs of Reform Judaism.

Other congregations also instituted reform ideas. In Baltimore, Har Sinai Congregation began to use a prayer book that was originally published by the Hamburg Temple in Germany. In New York City, Congregation Emanu-El published its own prayer book.

The year 1885 was a turning point for the Reform movement. A leading Reform rabbi, Kaufmann Kohler, called for a meeting of American Reform congregations in Pittsburgh. The beliefs of Reform Judaism that were established during that meeting became known as the Pittsburgh Platform. These ideas helped guide Reform Judaism for over fifty years.

My Books Spoke to Me

The following story is about Rabbi Isaac Mayer Wise. Rabbi Wise was a giant among leaders. He was born in Steingrub, Bohemia, in 1819. He immigrated to the United States in 1846, when he was twenty-seven years old.

When Rabbi Wise first came to the United States with his wife and baby, he had only two dollars. He was soon chosen to lead Congregation Beth El in Albany, New York. He worked hard to educate his congregation about Judaism and democracy.

Rabbi Wise felt that with the right education and freedom, all people could learn to love and respect one another. He wanted people who belonged to different congregations to feel a sense of unity with all Jews.

In 1854, Isaac Mayer Wise became the rabbi of B'nai Yeshurun Congregation in Cincinnati, Ohio. While he occupied this pulpit, Rabbi Wise tried out his ideas. He introduced his own prayer book called Minhag America. *He thought that if this book were used in all synagogues, American Jews would feel more united.*

Rabbi Wise traveled far and wide to make his ideas about unity known to American Jews. Wherever he went, he also spoke about the political rights that our Constitution guarantees the citizens of America. He was particularly concerned when he heard reports about anti-Semitism. He also spoke out against missionaries who tried to convert Jews.

Rabbi Isaac Mayer Wise.

In 1873, Rabbi Wise's dreams were fulfilled when he helped found the Union of American Hebrew Congregations. The purpose of this organization was to unite the various congregations in the United States. Two years later, he established Hebrew Union College in Cincinnati. It is the oldest existing rabbinical seminary in North America.

Isaac Mayer Wise died in 1900, at the age of eighty-one. The synagogues that had accepted his leadership became part of the Reform movement in America.

On the Shabbat before Rosh Hashanah in 1850, Rabbi Isaac Mayer Wise of Congregation Beth El in Albany, New York, approached the pulpit to give his weekly sermon. As he adjusted his glasses, he realized that the *shamash*, the official who ran the day-to-day affairs of the synagogue, was standing beside him. The *shamash* had an angry look on his face. He waved a piece of paper.

The *shamash* said, "You are not to preach today."

"Sir," Rabbi Wise answered, "what do you mean?"

"I have in my hand a notice of excommunication written by a New York rabbi. You have been found guilty of violating Jewish law. You are relieved of your position as rabbi of Congregation Beth El."

"My dear *shamash*," Rabbi Wise retorted, "I know nothing about these charges. As for excommunication, who has given the rabbi in New York the authority to write such a notice? After Shabbat, we will discuss the charges. However, until there is a board meeting at which time I will be allowed to answer the charges against me, I consider myself the rabbi of this congregation."

"I tell you, you shall not preach today," the *shamash* shouted, angrily shoving the paper in front of the rabbi.

With that, the *shamash* and several members of the congregation left the synagogue. Rabbi Wise looked at the rest of the congregants, who were now shouting, "Speak, Rabbi, speak." He proceeded to give his prepared sermon.

That evening, there was much excitement in the rabbi's home. People came and went, expressing their views about the incident. Rabbi Wise learned that a number of congregants believed he had violated some of the Jewish laws.

"You are innocent, Rabbi," his large group of faithful friends consoled him. "How could they invent such ridiculous charges?"

"I am afraid that those who oppose my ideas to reform Judaism want to harm me," Rabbi Wise said. "But I shall try to ignore what has happened today, and I shall continue my work until the synagogue board meets."

A few days later, on the first morning of Rosh Hashanah, the synagogue was full. Everyone had heard what had occurred the Shabbat before, and there was much whispering among the congregants.

Isaac Mayer Wise stepped up to the pulpit. He wished everyone *Leshanah Tovah* and announced that the services were about to begin. People quieted down and concentrated on the beautiful words of the Rosh Hashanah prayers.

Soon it was time to take the Torah out of the ark. Rabbi Wise opened the doors of the *Aron Hakodesh* and was about to lift the Torah. The president of the congregation stood at his side. Suddenly, the president lifted his fist and struck Rabbi Wise. The stunned rabbi reeled backward, almost losing his balance.

"How dare you profane the holiday in this manner?" Rabbi Wise exclaimed.

Shouting erupted from all sides. Many of the rabbi's friends rushed to his aid. Someone ran for the police. By the time the police arrived, the congregation had spilled out into the street. People were arguing and fighting with one another. There was no choice but to close the synagogue and send everyone home.

Later, Rabbi Wise and his wife talked about the day's troubling events. "They are angry at me because I have introduced a confirmation service and a choir consisting of both men and women. It is not good to cause this kind of conflict," he said. "For the sake of the congregation, I should probably leave Beth El."

"But you have so many friends and admirers here," his wife answered. "Let us invite them to worship with us here in our home, since the synagogue is closed."

"You are right, my dear. We can set up benches, and the people who wish to come in peace may do so."

The next day, the rooms of Rabbi Wise's home were packed with people. The choir of the synagogue was there, and everyone joined in reciting the prayers. When Rabbi Wise preached his sermon asking for unity, several members of the congregation began to cry.

Within a few days, the entire city knew of the events that had occurred in the synagogue on Rosh Hashanah. Rabbi Wise was upset. He did not know what to do. He needed time to think and read. The rabbi went to his study. He wondered whether he should quit the rabbinate. As he sat deep in thought, his eyes fell upon the hundreds of volumes that lined the walls. He closed his eyes and fell asleep. The holy books seemed to talk to him.

"Look at us," they said. "We are the Holy Scriptures of Judaism. You have been a faithful friend to us. Are you going to forsake us now? Where is your enthusiasm and your love for the people of Israel?"

"But my ideas have created a terrible conflict . . ."

"You must hold fast to your dreams," the books replied.

"Yes," the rabbi answered, "I have the holy task of teaching Judaism. I cannot forsake my dream of uniting Israel."

Rabbi Wise spoke so loudly that his wife rushed into the room. "What is the matter?" she cried. "You look so pale."

"Do not worry," the rabbi calmed her. "I had a wonderful dream. My books spoke to me. They told me that I should go on teaching. Let us call our friends who worshiped here on Rosh Hashanah. Together, we will organize a new synagogue. We will call it Anshe Emeth Congregation because those who have stood by me are people of truth."

B'nai Yeshurun Congregation, in Cincinnati, Ohio, was founded in 1840. It is now known as the Isaac M. Wise Temple.

Rebecca Gratz

Once upon a time, in the early nineteenth century, there lived a very beautiful woman. Her manner was gracious, and she looked like a princess. People came from far and near to talk with her and to be near her. Famous painters wanted to paint her portrait. People who had never met her praised her beauty and good deeds, for her fame had spread beyond her country to far-off lands.

Does this sound like a fairy tale? Actually, it is the story of Rebecca Gratz of Philadelphia, Pennsylvania. She was born in 1781, one of twelve children of Michael Gratz, a successful colonial merchant. Many stories and legends are told about Rebecca Gratz.

Rebecca enjoyed entertaining famous writers in her home. She became a friend of the popular American writer Washington Irving, the author of "The Legend of Sleepy Hollow." A story is told that once on a trip to England, Irving spoke of her to his friend Sir Walter Scott, the famous English novelist.

At that time, Sir Walter Scott was thinking about writing a new book called *Ivanhoe*. One of the characters in *Ivanhoe* was a beautiful dark-eyed Jewish girl named Rebecca. Some people have suggested that Scott's fictional Rebecca was based on Rebecca Gratz.

Rebecca spent her life performing *mitzvot* and *gemilut chasadim*—good deeds and acts of loving-kindness—and caring for her fellow human beings. She organized soci-

Rebecca Gratz.

eties to help poor Jewish women and to care for Jewish orphan children. But most of all, she dedicated herself to Jewish education in the United States.

The Jewish communities of America at that time did not have trained rabbis and teachers, as we do today. In 1838, Rebecca Gratz organized the first Jewish Sunday school in the United States. Because Rebecca had difficulty finding textbooks for her curriculum, she wrote much of the material herself. She served as principal of the Sunday school she founded until she was well into her eighties. By the time she died in 1869, at the age of eighty-eight, there were rabbis and teachers throughout America.

Isaac Leeser

Isaac Leeser.

"Very shy and lovable" was how people described Isaac Leeser, *chazan* of Congregation Mikveh Israel in Philadelphia during the years 1829 to 1850. Despite the fact that Leeser was a retiring person, he was one of the most important Jewish leaders of his time.

Isaac Leeser immigrated from Germany to Richmond, Virginia, when he was a teenager. At the age of twenty-three, he was elected *chazan* of Congregation Mikveh Israel. Leeser was concerned that the Jews of the United States did not know enough about Judaism. Books about Judaism were not printed in America. Most prayer books came from Europe and did not have an English translation. Leeser felt that if more books were printed in English, American Jews would be more observant.

Isaac Leeser began to write and publish books on Jewish subjects. He translated the Bible into English. He also wrote a translation of the prayer book. In addition, Isaac Leeser printed textbooks for the students who attended Rebecca Gratz's Sunday school.

Leeser published a monthly magazine called *The Occident*. The magazine was very popular. It contained information about what was happening in the small Jewish communities throughout the United States. To gather the information, Leeser traveled to many cities, where he was welcomed as a guest preacher.

Leeser strongly believed that if the Jews of America were going to keep their Jewish identity, changes had to be made in the organization of Jewish life. He insisted on giving regular weekly sermons, something that had not been done before. He also wanted Jewish students to be educated in Jewish-sponsored schools.

Most of all, he was concerned with the fact that there were few rabbis and teachers in the United States. As a result, he organized Maimonides College, which taught young people how to serve the religious needs of the American Jewish community. The college only lasted for six years, but it set a pattern for future colleges of this kind.

Chazan Leeser continued to influence the growth of Judaism in America throughout his life. He left Congregation Mikveh Israel in 1850, and in 1857, he became the leader of Beth El Emeth Congregation in Philadelphia until his death in 1868. His greatest hope was that all congregations begin to worship in the same way, regardless of the different customs that their members had brought with them from Europe.

SYNAGOGUES OF THE UNITED STATES

A regular feature of *The Occident* was news about various synagogues throughout the United States. As the editor of the magazine, Chazan Leeser visited many of these groups. News dispatches about some of the synagogues he visited appear below.

October 1845

I have just returned from a visit to Beth Shalome Congregation in Norfolk, Virginia. What a wonderful occasion was celebrated by the community. A new Torah scroll was delivered just in time for the High Holidays. There was a joyful procession amid much singing of psalms as the Torah was delivered to the ark. One of the newly arrived members is acting as the *shochet* for the community. Now there is no problem in settling in Norfolk because a family can have kosher meat in their home.

November 1845

As my readers know, I first arrived in this country at the age of seventeen and went to my uncle's home in Richmond. Recently, I returned for a visit. How the Jewish community has grown. There are now two congregations—the original Spanish Portuguese synagogue and a new one made up of Ashkenazim. The *chazan* of the Ashkenazic synagogue informs me that he intends to give his sermons in English. This will help the members learn English and become part of America. I am personally pleased with this idea.

September 1847

What a glorious trip I have had to New York City. Congregation Shearith Israel continues to lead the way in setting an example for Jewish behavior. The ladies of the synagogue sew clothes for the poor. The congregation does not miss a chance to help other synagogues when they need money. The good officers of the synagogue have organized a Jewish day school. In this time when so many of our people send their children to church schools for lack of a better place, Congregation Shearith Israel has a thriving school.

The newly organized Reform congregation has bought a church and intends to convert it into a temple. There is much activity in this group. Many of the members meet often to read and discuss the latest books.

I am pleased to report that there are now over a dozen and a half congregations in New York. If only the officers of these groups would take time to meet together to discuss their various projects. Think of what unity there would be among our people.

December 1851

Synagogues are being built all over this country. One of the most beautiful new buildings, I am pleased to write, is in Louisville, Kentucky. It bears the name of Adath Israel Congregation. When I delivered my sermon, what a pleasure it was to see that all of the seats were filled. Unfortunately, I was told of a rift in the group. It seems that some of the members who come from Poland have left the congregation to form a new one of their own. Adath Israel Congregation is now made up of only German immigrants. Again, I appeal for unity among our congregations. When Jews live together, there should be no disharmony in synagogue worship.

Fill in the blanks.

1. Name the German Jewish scholar who believed that the Jews living in the ghettos needed to learn the ways of the modern world._____

2. Describe the goals of Israel Jacobson's school in Seesen, Germany._____
   _____
   _____

3. In which German city was the first Reform temple built?_____

4. Why was there a need for change in the synagogues of the early 1800s?_____
   _____
   _____

5. List three reforms that Isaac Mayer Wise instituted.

   a. _____

   b. _____

   c. _____

6. Name three other Reform congregations that were established during the early
   1800s._____
   _____
   _____

7. Isaac Mayer Wise moved from Albany, New York, to lead B'nai Yeshurun Congregation in_____.

8. Name two major institutions that Isaac Mayer Wise helped found._____
   _____

9. _____ established the first Jewish Sunday school.

10. _____ wrote about synagogues that he visited on his travels and published Jewish books in English.

DISCUSSION

1. Isaac Mayer Wise was dedicated to Jewish unity. Define the meaning of Jewish unity. Discuss the importance of Jewish unity.

2. Why do you think that the members of Congregation Beth El in Albany were upset with some of Rabbi Wise's reforms? Can you think of some constructive ways in which they could have voiced their concerns?

ACTIVITIES

1. With which national synagogue organization is your synagogue affiliated? Research the history of this organization.

2. Write a police report about what happened on Rosh Hashanah at Congregation Beth El, or make believe that you are a news announcer on television and write a news report about what took place.

3. Identify a local Jewish leader. Interview that person. Ask that leader about his or her goals, how he or she tries to accomplish them, and whether he or she has met with resistance. Write a report based on your interview.

4. Visit different synagogues in your community. Write a description of each synagogue for a special issue of *The Occident,* to be published by your class.

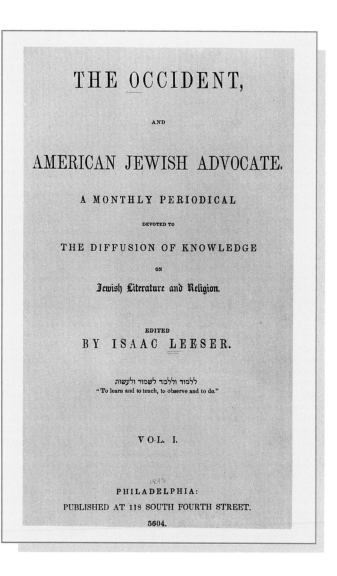

THE OCCIDENT,

AND

AMERICAN JEWISH ADVOCATE.

A MONTHLY PERIODICAL

DEVOTED TO

THE DIFFUSION OF KNOWLEDGE

ON

Jewish Literature and Religion.

EDITED

BY ISAAC LEESER.

ללמוד וללמד לשמור ולעשות
"To learn and to teach, to observe and to do."

VOL. I.

PHILADELPHIA:
PUBLISHED AT 118 SOUTH FOURTH STREET.
5604.

C H A P T E R 8

WAR BETWEEN THE STATES

LINKS IN HISTORY
Civil War

By the mid-1800s, it had become obvious that the Northern and Southern states seriously disagreed on several important issues. Most Northerners felt that slavery was evil. Most Southerners, on the other hand, regarded their slaves as property and as a necessary part of their life. As each new state joined the United States, the main question was whether the state would be a free state or a slave state.

The Soldier's Dream of Home by Max Rosenthal, the official illustrator for the U.S. Military Commission during the Civil War.

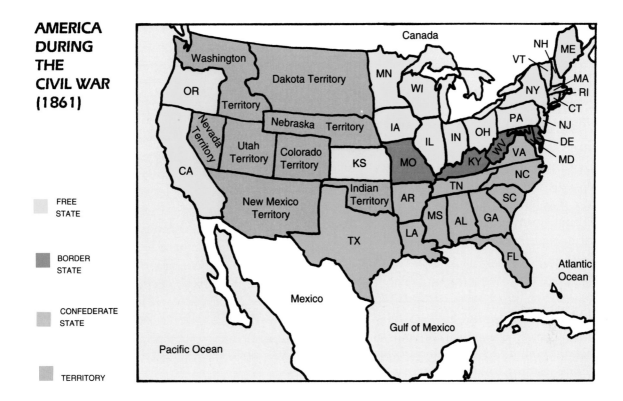

AMERICA DURING THE CIVIL WAR (1861)

FREE STATE

BORDER STATE

CONFEDERATE STATE

TERRITORY

The people who wanted freedom for slaves were called **abolitionists**, from the word *abolish*. Some of these people were from the South, but most were Northerners who worked hard to get their message of freedom heard.

By 1861, when Abraham Lincoln became president of the United States, the arguments were so intense that the country was about to break apart. The Southern states felt that they had the right to break away from the Union. They did not accept Abraham Lincoln as their president. The Northern states felt that a strong central government was what the country needed.

In December 1860, South Carolina left the Union. It was soon followed by other Southern states. They formed a new government and called it the Confederate States of America. Abraham Lincoln strongly opposed this action.

On April 12, 1861, a battle between Southern and Northern troops took place at Fort Sumter in Charleston, South Carolina. The Civil War had begun. It lasted four years and finally ended on April 9, 1865.

During this period, people who had close ties with both the North and South were forced to choose sides. Often, families were split apart. Sometimes, fathers and sons fought one another. Thousands of soldiers died. Abraham Lincoln was assassinated. In the end, the Union was preserved. The United States had to rebuild a war-torn land. It was a trying time for our country.

THE JEWISH EXPERIENCE

In the year 1850, there were about fifty thousand Jews living in the United States. During the next ten years, about one hundred thousand more Jews immigrated to these shores. They came at a time when this country was involved in a great debate about the issue of slavery. The United States was on the brink of civil war, and each new immigrant had to make a personal decision about the issue of slavery.

THE NORTH AGAINST THE SOUTH
Many of the Jews who immigrated here during the 1850s were from countries in Europe in which uprisings and revolutions were going on. A large number of the young men had fought for freedom in Germany. The majority of new Jewish immigrants settled in the Northern states. These people were convinced that no one's freedom was secure in a land that allowed slavery to exist.

The Southern states also had a large Jewish population. The families of many of these Jews had been in America for generations. Like their non-Jewish neighbors, some of these people owned plantations and slaves. They felt that slaves were their private property, and they were ready to fight to hold on to their property. They resented the Northerners' telling them what to do.

RABBIS SPEAK OUT
The rabbis of the various Jewish congregations in the United States used their pulpits to express their ideas for and against slavery. You might think that the rabbis who lived in the North

Rabbi David Einhorn.

were all on the side of the abolitionists and that those who lived in the South were in favor of slavery. This was not always the case.

One rabbi, Morris Raphall of New York City, believed that the Bible gave people the right to own slaves. He pointed out, however, that the difference between biblical slavery and American slavery was the just way in which Jewish law treated slaves. His views were printed in newspapers and pamphlets throughout the United States.

Many Jews disagreed with Rabbi Raphall. The most vocal abolitionist viewpoint was that of Rabbi David Einhorn of Baltimore, Maryland. Maryland was a "border state," one of a group of states that sympathized with its Southern neighbors but chose not to secede from the Union.

Rabbi Einhorn spoke out strongly against the evils of slavery. He reminded his congregation that Jews were once slaves in Egypt. He said that as long as there was slavery in the land, no one was free.

Rabbi Einhorn made many enemies among the groups in Baltimore that were in favor of slavery. His congregation asked him to stop bringing up "excitable issues," but he kept on preaching his message of freedom. For a time, young men from his congregation stood guard in front of the rabbi's house because they feared for his life. One night, Rabbi Einhorn and his family had to flee to Philadelphia because they had learned that a mob was preparing to harm them.

Another rabbi, Sabato Morais, who was Isaac Leeser's successor at Congregation Mikveh Israel in Philadelphia, also spoke out in favor of the Union. Rabbi Morais, a Sephardi, came from Italy, where he had fought for political freedom. Seeing that his new country was splitting apart, he spoke out on every possible occasion for democracy and for the need to stay united.

THE CIVIL WAR

In 1861, war broke out. Thousands of Jews enlisted in the armies of both sides. They fought with much courage, and many of them were heroes. Rabbi Arnold Fischel petitioned the Union for a change in the chaplaincy law, which stated that only Christians could be chaplains in the armed forces. Rabbi Fischel felt that the law was unjust, particularly since so many Jews were serving in the army. The law was changed, and Ferdinand Sarner, formerly the rabbi of Brith Kodesh Synagogue in Rochester, New York, became the country's first Jewish chaplain.

PRESIDENT ABRAHAM LINCOLN

During his term in office, Lincoln was very friendly to the Jews. President Lincoln died on April 14, 1865, shot by an assassin's bullet. It was the fifth day of Passover. The war was over, and the Jews of New York and Philadelphia had just sent 5,000 pounds of *matzot* to the Jews of Savannah. That morning, Rabbi Max Lilienthal of Cincinnati put aside his prepared sermon and spoke of the slain president. He said, "Indeed a great man has fallen in Israel." Jews all over the United States wept as they heard the sad news from their rabbis.

A portrait of President Abraham Lincoln, painted by Solomon Nunes Carvalho.

General Order Number Eleven

Do you know the meaning of the word scapegoat? *A scapegoat is a person who gets blamed when something goes wrong, even if that person is not at fault. People often blame other people who cannot defend themselves. Jews have frequently been scapegoats, even in the United States.*

In the year 1862, as the Union army began to gain an edge in the fighting, an ugly incident occurred in the Jewish communities of Kentucky, Tennessee, and Mississippi. The Jews who lived in these states became scapegoats.

Following in the path of the Union army came traders, eager to buy cotton and resell it in the North. To do this, they had to smuggle the cotton, which is a product of the South, into the North. These acts were a violation of the blockade instituted by the North. With the outbreak of the Civil War, factories in the North that had depended on Southern cotton had had their supplies cut off. Now that the Southern states were being retaken by the North, the Northern factories were willing to pay high prices for cotton.

Thousands of traders became rich buying and selling cotton. General Ulysses S. Grant was annoyed that the traders were taking advantage of a wartime situation. He was also angry that there were so many traders. He felt that they were interfering with the movement of his army. He wanted the traders expelled from the area.

Although some of the traders were Jews, most were not. However, it was easy to lay the blame on the Jews because many of them were immigrants. They stood out because of their foreign ways and accents. An order was issued under General Grant's name that expelled all Jews from Kentucky, Tennessee, and Mississippi.

In the story you are about to read, you will see how the Jews defended their rights.

The wharf along the Ohio River in Paducah, Kentucky, in the final days of the year 1862 was a chaotic scene. Union soldiers were pushing people onto the riverboat that was anchored alongside the dock. A young mother ran down the gangplank crying, "My baby, where is my baby?" A soldier barred her way. "Madam, you may not get off the boat. We are trying to load it."

"But I don't see my baby."

"Is this your child, Madam?" a young soldier approached the upset mother and almost threw the tiny infant at her. "She was left among the suitcases that are being loaded."

"Thank God," cried the mother, clutching her screaming child.

"Now go back on board the boat," the guard told her. "We must lift anchor soon."

At the far end of the wharf, more people were waiting to embark. One of them, Cesar Kaskel, a respected resident of Paducah, was arguing with an officer.

"I would like to know why the Jews of this area are being deported to Cincinnati," he said. "We have done nothing wrong."

The officer replied gruffly, "I do not have to give you a reason. Just get on line. We leave in half an hour."

"Officer," Cesar went on, "may I at least sell my horse and buggy? I will need the money to provide for my family."

"You have nothing to sell. This horse and buggy now belong to us," the officer replied.

Cesar persisted, "We thirty Jews of Paducah have been ordered to leave town in just twenty-four hours, and as yet no one has given us a reason for this outrage."

The officer looked at Cesar and snarled, "You are being sent upstream because you are Jews and are of no use to either the Union or the Confederacy. Jews have been trading cotton against the orders of General Grant. By his order, all Jews are being expelled from this area."

"Sir, we may be in the midst of a civil war, but this outrage will not go unnoticed," Cesar replied. "It is true that some Jews are trading against the orders of the army, but they are a small minority. Expel only the lawbreakers, not the entire

community. I shall go all the way to the White House to plead our case." Realizing that further talk was useless, Cesar joined the line of refugees.

As soon as the party of Jews reached Cincinnati, Cesar Kaskel wasted no time. He wrote letters to Jewish newspapers and sent telegrams to let the Jewish community know about the unjust order that General Ulysses S. Grant had issued. Then he rushed to Washington, D.C., where he hoped to speak to President Abraham Lincoln. Congressman Gurley of Ohio secured an immediate appointment with the president.

A grave but smiling Lincoln greeted the two men. "What brings you to Washington during wartime, my dear Mr. Kaskel?" Lincoln asked.

"Sir," Cesar replied, "it grieves me to disturb you during these troubled times, but a terrible thing has befallen the members of my faith who reside in Kentucky, because of an order issued by General Grant. My people are being expelled from their homes." Cesar showed President Lincoln a copy of General Order Number Eleven.

Holly Springs, Miss.
December 17, 1862
The Jews as a class, violating every regulation of trade . . . are hereby expelled from . . . [Kentucky, Tennessee, and Mississippi] within twenty-four hours from the receipt of this order.

Post commanders will see that all of this class of people be furnished passes and required to leave, and any one returning . . . will be arrested and held in confinement . . . as prisoners.
By order of Major-General U.S. Grant.

J. A. Rawlins
Assistant Adjutant-General

"I have no knowledge of this order, and I am very distressed that it was given," Lincoln exclaimed. "Jews fighting for the Union have brought honor to our nation. I shall write to General Grant immediately, informing him that this order is contrary to the freedoms the Union so highly prizes and that it must be stopped. The children of Israel shall not be driven from their homes."

Cesar smiled and said, "We came to Father Abraham asking for protection, and you have not disappointed us."

"And you shall have this protection at once," Lincoln replied, as Cesar Kaskel and Congressman Gurley rose to leave.

President Lincoln immediately sent a telegram to the general-in-chief of the army, Henry Halleck. After General Halleck read the telegram, he sent the following message to General Grant.

General John A. Rawlins, General Ulysses S. Grant, and Colonel T. S. Bowers.

War Department
January 4, 1863
Major-General Grant
Holly Strings, Mississippi

A paper purporting to be General Order Number Eleven, issued by you December 17, has been presented here. By its terms, it expels all Jews from your department. If such an order has been issued, it will be immediately revoked.

H. W. Halleck
General-in-Chief

A joyful Cesar Kaskel delivered the news to the Jewish refugees in Cincinnati. "My friends," he told them happily, "President Lincoln has lived up to his name, Honest Abe. He was very upset when he heard that we were expelled from our homes. He has informed General Grant that the order is unjust. We are free to return to our homes without further delay."

Judah Philip Benjamin

Some people who are born Jewish do not want to be thought of as Jews. They do not associate themselves with the Jewish community. Yet much to their surprise, their neighbors consider them to be Jews.

This is what happened to Judah P. Benjamin, a very powerful official in the government of the Confederacy during the Civil War. Judah was born in the Virgin Islands in 1811, into a Sephardic family. His family eventually moved to Charleston, South Carolina. He was a brilliant student and entered Yale at the age of fourteen. Instead of graduating, however, Judah moved to New Orleans to study law. He became a successful lawyer and was soon able to buy a large plantation. He married a Catholic woman from Louisiana, and although he did not convert to Catholicism, he never practiced Judaism.

The state of Louisiana elected Judah to the United States Senate. He left Washington when the Confederacy was formed. He believed in slavery and the right of the individual states to secede from the Union. Jefferson Davis, the president of the Confederacy, was Judah's close friend. Davis asked Judah to serve in his government as attorney general. Judah then became secretary of war and secretary of state of the Confederacy. Despite Judah's loyalty to the Confederate cause, however, many Southerners disliked him because he was Jewish.

Judah P. Benjamin left the South in the final days of the Civil War and made his way to England, where he resumed his law career. He became successful and earned a fortune by selling law books that he wrote. The "handsome, mysterious, and gifted" Judah P. Benjamin died in 1884.

Judah P. Benjamin, whose face is pictured on the Confederate two-dollar bill, was secretary of state and later secretary of war of the Confederate States.

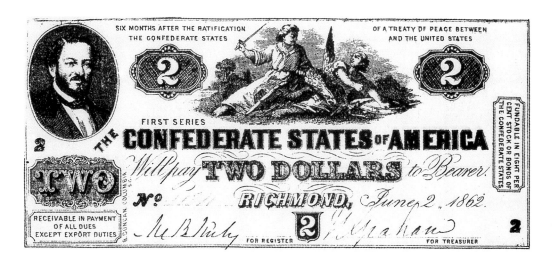

How They Lived

American Jews fought for both sides in the Civil War. Records show that at least 6,000 Jewish soldiers served in the Union army, and 1,200 served in the Confederate army. Six Jewish soldiers who fought for the Union received the Congressional Medal of Honor.

The following quote is from the autobiography of August Bondi. Before the Civil War, Bondi worked with John Brown, an abolitionist. When this passage was written, Bondi was a soldier in the Union army.

October 25, 1862:

To my knowledge there were three *Yehudim* [Jews] in the Fifth Kansas Cavalry: Marcus Wittenberg, Simon Wolf, and myself. Some time in July, I accosted [stopped] Wittenberg asking, "Are you not a Jew?" He answered, "I'm a Hungarian; my folks live near Lawrence." . . . A few days after that, Wittenberg fell sick and was taken to the hospital, . . . where he died. A few days after his death, his chum John Emile . . . brought me some letters . . . written in a language unknown to him. There were letters from his [Wittenberg's] parents, written in Hebrew, . . . informing him of the date of Rosh Hashanah and Yom Kippur. Now, if Wittenberg had not denied his being a Jew, I would have seen to him daily and possibly saved him.

Simon Wolf, a Jewish lawyer who lived in Washington, D.C., appealed to President Lincoln on behalf of a young Jewish soldier who had been condemned to death because he had deserted. This is a quote from a book written by Mr. Wolf.

A letter came, and it stated that a young soldier, American born, of Jewish faith, had been condemned to be shot, . . . the next morning. . . . It seemed this soldier could not get a furlough. His mother, who was on her deathbed, had begged for his return . . . to give him a parting blessing. . . . He went home, was arrested, and condemned to be shot.

[A hasty meeting was arranged with President Lincoln.] It was two o'clock in the morning before we reached the president.

American Jews fought on both sides during the Civil War.

The president walked up and down with his hands hanging by his side. . . . He listened with deep attention. . . . I said, "Mr. President, you will pardon me for a moment. What would you have done under similar circumstances if your dying mother had summoned you to her bedside to receive her last message?" . . . He stopped, touched the bell; his secretary came in; he ordered a telegram to be sent to stop the execution.

Confederate soldier Major Raphael J. Moses, the head of a Sephardic Jewish family that had lived in the South for generations, left us a sad diary entry about finding his dying nineteen-year-old son, Albert Moses Luria, among the wounded in a Richmond hospital. He had gone to the hospital looking for his nephew, Moses, who had also been wounded. He wrote:

. . . as I was interested in the fate of my nephew, I went to the hospital where Col. Clayton informed me the ambulance had carried young Moses. . . . The ward was pointed out to me and I passed among the wounded. I saw some ladies standing by a cot and heard one of them say: "What a handsome young man!" I crossed over to the cot, and my shock was beyond my power of expression when I saw my son Albert lying unconscious, never recognizing me. He died that night from loss of blood.

Write **True** or **False** next to each of the following statements. Then rewrite the false statements to make them true.

1. Rabbi David Einhorn stopped giving antislavery sermons when his Baltimore synagogue requested him to do so._____

2. By 1850, there were one hundred and fifty thousand Jews living in the United States._____

3. All of the rabbis in America spoke out against slavery._____

4. Rabbi Arnold Fischel fought to change the law that barred rabbis as chaplains.

_____

5. Some Jews owned slaves in the days of the Bible._____

6. Most of the cotton traders in the South were Jewish immigrants._____

7. President Lincoln did not approve the order to expel the Jewish traders from Kentucky._____

8. The Jewish cotton traders were scapegoats because many of them were immigrants._____

9. Most of the Jews living in the South during the Civil War were recent immigrants._____

10. Six Union soldiers of the Jewish faith received the Congressional Medal of Honor._____

DISCUSSION

1. When Ulysses S. Grant ran for president in 1868, there were many debates about General Order Number Eleven. The following are some of the arguments that were heard at the time.

a. "The Jews were forcing up the price of cotton unfairly."

"You are wrong. Some Jews may have been involved, but many other people were also trading illegally. Some say that General Grant's own father was involved in cotton trading across enemy lines. Jews are often the scapegoats and are made to take the blame in bad times."

_____

_____

_____

_____

b. "Grant says that he did not write that order."
"So why doesn't he say so publicly? Perhaps he is covering up for someone on his staff who wrote it in his name."

_____

_____

_____

_____

c. "How will he treat the Jews if he is elected president?"
"I think he will try to be fair to the Jews in order to make this ugly incident part of the past."

_____

_____

_____

_____

In the spaces provided, comment on each of the above arguments. If you had been able to vote in 1868, how do you think you would have felt about Grant as a presidential candidate?

2. Reread the quote from August Bondi, which appears on page 86. Discuss your reaction to the last sentence: "Now, if Wittenberg had not denied his being a Jew, I would have seen to him daily and possibly saved him."

3. Read the story of the Exodus in the *Tanach*. Compare the lives of the Jewish slaves in Egypt with the lives of the African slaves in America. Have your teacher or rabbi explain how the situations were similar and how they were different.

ACTIVITIES

1. Write a short play about Albert Moses Luria's death.

2. Write the first chapter of a book that tells how the Jews of Paducah, Kentucky, spent the twenty-four hours they were given to leave their homes.

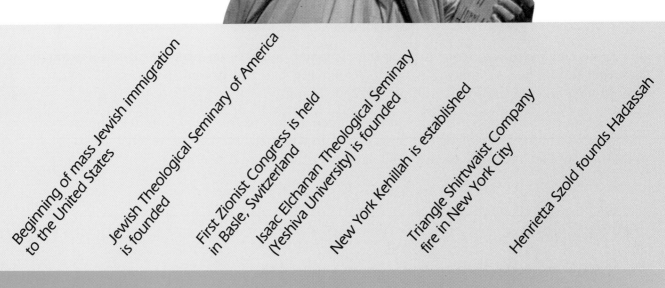

Beginning of mass Jewish immigration to the United States

Jewish Theological Seminary of America is founded

First Zionist Congress is held in Basle, Switzerland

Isaac Elchanan Theological Seminary (Yeshiva University) is founded

New York Kehillah is established

Triangle Shirtwaist Company fire in New York City

Henrietta Szold founds Hadassah

1881   **1886**   **1897**   **1908**   **1911**   **1912**

BY THE MILLIONS, THEY CAME

UNIT IV

From 1881 to 1924, millions of Jews from all parts of Europe and Asia immigrated to America. Why did they leave lands in which they and their ancestors had lived for hundreds of years? How did they manage to settle down in America, establish homes and businesses, and build synagogues and Jewish centers?

You will learn that there were two immigrations. One is the story of the Ashkenazic Jewish immigration. The other is the story of the immigration of Sephardic Jews. You will find out how the immigrants made a living and how they struggled to bring about changes in the workplace that have benefited all Americans. You will also learn about Conservative and Orthodox Judaism in America.

Finally, you will read about how American Jews became Zionists and helped their fellow Jews immigrate to Palestine. Read carefully because for many of you, this is the time that the history of your own families in this country began.

1914	1917	1918	1920	1922	1924
World War I begins	Russian Revolution / America enters World War I	Armistice—World War I ends	Women win the right to vote	Jewish Institute of Religion is founded	Strict laws restricting immigration are passed by Congress

CHAPTER 9

WAVE AFTER WAVE OF PEOPLE

LINKS IN HISTORY

A Ticket to America, Please

In 1860, there were thirty-one million people living in the United States. By 1891, immigrants to the United States had swelled the population to sixty-three million, and many more were to arrive in the next twenty-five years. People came from all parts of Europe and Asia. What prompted all of these people to make the difficult journey to America?

Many people living in Europe and Asia were eager to leave their homes and find new ones. Living conditions in their countries were often very poor. Land and jobs were scarce. Governments were frequently cruel and uncaring, and religious persecution was widespread. People heard that America was a land of opportunity and freedom.

In 1914, a great war began in Europe. Within a few years, the United States was drawn into this conflict. The war was called World War I. Although no battles were fought in the United States, many Americans lost their lives on the battlefields of Europe. As the battles raged on, the population of Europe was caught in the middle of the war.

Immigration, which had continued in huge numbers right up to the beginning of World War I, practically stopped during the war. America and its allies were victorious, and on November 11, 1918, the war was over. Immigration to the United States, particularly from the countries that had been affected by the war, now began again.

But after the war, Americans were less willing to give shelter to people who wanted to live here. The returning soldiers needed jobs, and they did not want to compete for work with immigrants. Many Americans now wanted to keep to themselves and have nothing to do with people from other countries.

In 1917, Congress passed a law called the Literacy Test Act. This law required that immigrants be able to read in their own language or in English before they could enter this country. Since many Europeans and Asians had no schooling, this law reduced immigration.

By 1924, more laws had been passed. These laws put a limit, or **quota**, on the number of people that were allowed to enter the United States from each country. These laws further reduced the number of new immigrants.

In 1884, France presented the United States with a gift. It was the Statue of Liberty, which now stands in New York harbor. Emma Lazarus, a young woman born into a Sephardic New York family, wrote a poem called "The New Colossus." In 1903, several years after her death, her poem was inscribed on a plaque just inside the entrance to the statue. The last stanza reads:

> Give me your tired, your poor,
> Your huddled masses yearning to breathe
>   free,
> The wretched refuse of your teeming shore.
> Send these, the homeless, tempest-tossed
>   to me,
> I lift my lamp beside the golden door!

THE JEWISH EXPERIENCE

Jews have lived in parts of Russia for over one thousand years. The czars who ruled Russia disliked their Jewish subjects and often persecuted them. In the 1700s, Poland, which had a large Jewish population, was split up among Austria, Russia, and Prussia. As a result, Russia's Jewish population swelled to almost one million. The czars forced the Jews to live in one region of the country, which was called the **Pale of Settlement**. Many of them lived in small towns and villages called **shtetls**.

IMMIGRATION OF ASHKENAZIC JEWS

In 1827, Czar Nicholas I enacted laws that forced thousands of Jewish young men to join the army at about the age of twelve. Some of them stayed in the army for as long as twenty-five years. They were made to eat nonkosher food and to violate the Sabbath. Some were tortured until they converted to Christianity.

Alexander II succeeded Nicholas I. He tried to give his people some of the freedoms enjoyed by other European nations. But when he was assassinated in 1881, his son, Alexander III, did away with many of the liberal laws that his father had passed.

The Russian peasants were oppressed and angry. In order to cool the peasants' anger, the government made the Jews scapegoats. By this time, some Jews had moved to large cities, and others were attending colleges. The czar ordered them to go back to the Pale of Settlement. Once they were there, he drove families out of the villages into the larger towns, where they were forced to live in ghettos.

The Russian peasants were told that the Jews were responsible for their poverty and for the death of Czar Alexander II. As a result, the peasants rioted and attacked the Jews. These attacks were called **pogroms**. Some Jews were killed, and many were injured. A large number of homes were destroyed. Fearing for their lives, thousands of Jewish families hastily gathered their belongings and made their way across Europe to ports in Germany. There they booked passage to foreign countries. Some of them went to England and France. Others stayed in Germany. Still others left for Australia, South Africa, and Canada. A few went to the land of Israel. But the majority chose to go to the United States.

THE JOURNEY TO AMERICA

On board ships bound for America, the poorest Jews slept in **steerage**, the cheapest and most crowded section of a boat. Many ate herring and bread, which they had brought with them so as not to violate the laws of *kashrut*.

The ships proceeded to ports along the Eastern seaboard. Later, some of them even went to Galveston, Texas. Jewish organizations hoped that the people who landed in places like Galveston would spread out into the less crowded areas of the country.

The largest growth in Jewish population occurred in New York City. With an average of about eight dollars in their pockets, millions of immigrants streamed into New York harbor. Immigration officers examined them for diseases, asked them how much money they had, and decided whether or not to permit them to enter the United States.

Jews who arrived at Ellis Island had to undergo many exams before they were admitted into the United States. Ellis Island is now a museum dedicated to all the immigrants who passed through that entry point.

The Hebrew Immigrant Aid Society, known as HIAS, was established in 1909. It helped people pass through immigration at Ellis Island. HIAS worked to get immigrants jobs and gave them emergency funds for food and housing. Often the society also provided transportation to help the new arrivals join their families in other cities.

Between the years 1881 and 1924, as persecution and poverty continued in Russia, Poland, Hungary, and Romania, 2.3 million Jews made their way to America. In 1924, Congress passed laws limiting immigration to this country. Today, a museum on Ellis Island tells the story of these poor but hopeful newcomers who passed through on their way to the *Goldene Medina*, the "Golden Land."

SETTLING IN AMERICA Upon arriving in New York, most Jewish immigrants headed for the Lower East Side. There they found family or friends who had come from the same towns in Europe that they did. Like so many others who had arrived before, the new immigrants rented space in old, run-down **tenements**. At first, all they could afford was a room, or perhaps just a place on the floor. Many of the buildings were firetraps. They had steep staircases and few windows. The toilet was either in a long, narrow, dark hall or out in the backyard. Many families shared one bathroom.

Family and friends guided the immigrants through their confusing first days in the new country. This included helping

Many Jewish immigrant families lived in run-down, overcrowded tenements.

them find a job. Since most of the Jews came from areas that had few industries, they had no skills. They were offered work in **sweatshops**, where the pay was not more than seven to fifteen dollars per week for men, and less for women. Sweatshops were unsanitary and often overcrowded places where clothing was made. Men, women, and children sometimes sat at sewing machines in airless rooms for twelve hours a day.

A family that had many children and their own apartment would work at home. In the early morning, one member of the family would go to a cutting center to collect bundles of pieces to sew. The family sewed all day. In the evening, when the garments had been completed, payment was received based on the number of finished pieces. This kind of work became known as **piecework**. Having many children who could help sew was clearly an advantage.

OTHER WAYS TO MAKE A LIVING A few of the Jewish immigrants did not want to live in the crowded cities. They believed that Jews would regain their dignity as a people only if they became farmers. Because Jews in Europe had often been forbidden to own land and had frequently faced the risk of expulsion, they had never learned farming skills. Baron Maurice de Hirsch, a wealthy European Jewish philanthropist, donated money to set up agricultural and technical schools in America. One such colony, in Woodbine, New Jersey, became a successful farm. Other Jewish farms were started in Colorado, Kansas, and North Dakota.

DAILY LIFE Education was very important to the Jewish immigrants. As soon as they could, families enrolled their children in public schools, where they learned the English language. Some of the adults learned English from their children. Others went to night school after long hours at work. Soon some of the young adults were even attending the city colleges.

The public libraries were very popular places. Newspapers also played an important part in the lives of the immigrants. From the Yiddish newspapers, they found out about life around them. When they learned to read English, the English newspapers taught them about life in America.

As the immigrants became accustomed to America and began to better themselves, they had more time for entertainment. One of the most popular forms of entertainment was the theater. The plays were presented in Yiddish. People flocked to see their favorite stage shows and stars.

JEWISH EDUCATION Parents wanted their children to learn about Judaism. At this time, young children usually attended an afternoon school called a **cheder**, which is Hebrew for "room." The *cheder* was often a dirty, unheated room with hard benches and few books. The teacher spoke in Yiddish and was not usually trained to teach young children. Many children disliked going to *cheder*.

Soon schools called Talmud Torahs became popular. The teachers in these schools spoke English and were trained to instruct young children. The curriculum was similar to that of religious schools today. Children were taught Hebrew, Bible, Jewish history, customs and ceremonies, and Hebrew songs.

Yiddish theater was one of the most popular leisure-time activities of Jewish immigrants.

97

By Boat to Galveston, Texas

Hundreds of thousands of Jews came to America from Eastern Europe during the late 1800s and the early 1900s. The crowded Lower East Side in New York City was teeming with immigrants from dozens of countries.

In order to relieve the overcrowding in the large cities, a German Jewish philanthropist, Jacob Schiff, convinced the steamship lines to send people to ports in other parts of the country. The idea was that more jobs would be available to immigrants in other sections of the country.

In the following story, four friends set out for Galveston, Texas. Many immigrants actually experienced trips like the one described below. Years later, some of these people recorded their adventures in memoirs and letters.

Yossel, Shmuel, and Yankel were best friends. They lived with their families in Hozerkov, a small town in Russia near the city of Kiev. Their lives were poor but peaceful. Then they began hearing that pogroms were taking place in towns and cities across Russia. The people of Kishinev, a nearby town, had recently been victims of a horrible massacre. Jews had been slaughtered, and houses had been burnt to the ground.

When the news of this pogrom reached Hozerkov, the three boys and their parents met. With great fear, they discussed the future.

"Go to America," Yossel's father said. "You cannot stay here. Hozerkov might be next. You must get away as fast as you can."

"Papa, I will go only if Shmuel and Yankel go, too. They are my best friends, and I won't leave without them," Yossel answered.

Shmuel's mother began to cry. "Oy," she said, "what will become of him and us? We depend on him to help us make a living. He is strong and goes to the forest each day to carry wood for the woodchoppers."

"Now, now," Shmuel's father comforted her. "You know that it is dangerous for our boy to stay here."

"But what about you? How can I leave without you?" Yankel asked his parents.

"We will sell what little valuables we have," his father said, trying to sound hopeful. "That will provide you with just enough to get to America. America is a rich country. We hear that once you arrive, there are agents who will help you get a job. Do not worry about us. We are older. Perhaps the mobs will leave us alone. God willing, when you have made enough money, you will send for us. There is nothing left for us now in Russia."

At the last minute, Yossel's parents persuaded him to take along his sister, eight-year-old Shifra. "But Papa," Yossel said,

In 1903, the Kishinev pogrom left 50 Jews dead and 600 wounded.

"there is not enough money for the two of us. And Shifra is only a child. How will I support her?"

"Take her," Papa said firmly. "Her life is in danger here."

The boys, who ranged in age from seventeen to twenty-one, left Hozerkov in a hurry. The year was 1903. The four young people traveled across Europe for over a month. Their destination was Bremen, Germany, where they were to board the steamship the SS *Frankfurt*. By the time they reached Bremen, each boy had only about eight dollars in his pocket. They had begun the journey with more money, but they had used most of it on their long trip across Europe.

The SS *Frankfurt* was a large steamship. When the four youths first saw the ship proudly moored in the harbor, they were excited. But their excitement faded when they were led down into the crowded steerage section and shown where they were to sleep. The large space was partitioned into tiny cubicles, furnished with bunk beds stacked in groups of threes.

"Are we to sleep here?" Yankel asked the sailor who had led the way. The sailor, who spoke only German and did not understand Yiddish, pushed Yankel toward the cubicle.

"Yossel," Shifra whined, "there is no air in here. It smells awful. I miss Mama. Please take me home." Shifra began to cry.

"Don't cry, Shifra," Shmuel tried to comfort her. "We are going to a beautiful land. Some say the streets are paved with gold. As soon as we are settled, we will send for your mama and papa."

The steerage section filled up quickly, and soon the ship was on its way. At first, people were nice to one another.

"Where are you from?"

"Where are you going?"

"Do you have relatives in America? I hear this ship will stop in Baltimore, Maryland, and then in Galveston, Texas."

"Oy, where is Galveston, Texas? Are there Indians there?"

After only two days at sea, however, life became very difficult. Each morning, the passengers had to report to the ship's doctor. He gave them a quick examination and filled out a health card for each of them. Heaven help a passenger who felt ill. The doctor was so busy filling out health cards that he did not have the time to treat anyone who was sick.

By the end of the second day, the four travelers from Hozerkov had eaten all the food that kind Jews had given them in Bremen.

"What shall we do?" Yankel asked Shmuel.

"I hear that they have a kosher kitchen for steerage passengers. Let us go tonight and see if we can eat there," Shmuel replied.

At dinner, they followed the crowd to the dining room. It was a small crowded room, which only held about fifty people at a time. People were pushing to get in. When the boys and Shifra finally were able to find seats, they were given a bowl of potatoes, a little meat that smelled bad, and some bread and water.

"Yossel, there are worms in the bread," Shifra said to her brother. Yossel took the bread back to the kitchen crewman who had given it to them and tried to explain that the bread was not fit to eat. The crewman pushed Yossel and sneered, "Sit down. This is all you get."

That night, the steerage section was unbearably hot. The travelers went up to the deck to get some relief. Suddenly, sailors appeared with buckets of water.

"Go back to your places," they shouted, as they threw the water at the frightened passengers.

It took two weeks for the ship to cross the ocean and dock in Baltimore. Many people got off there, but the friends went on to Galveston, a journey of another ten days.

As the passengers left the ship, they were herded into rooms, where they were questioned about their plans for settling in America.

"How much money do you have?"

"What kind of work did you do in Russia?"

"Do you have relatives here? Do you have the promise of a job?"

Next, a doctor examined their eyes for trachoma and tested their muscles.

Yankel and Shmuel passed all the tests. Yes, they had enough money. No, they did

The immigrants aboard this ship were eager to begin their new life in Galveston, Texas.

not have family here, but they were strong and their muscles showed that they could do hard physical labor.

Yossel and Shifra were not so fortunate. The doctor told Yossel, "You are flat chested." This meant that he had no muscles.

To the question "How much money do you have?" Yossel replied, "Eight dollars."

To the question "How much money does the girl have?" he replied, "None."

"We are sorry but we cannot permit your sister to stay in the United States," an immigrant official told Yossel. "She will have to return to Bremen. You are not fit for hard work and would not be able to support her."

"I promised our parents that I would care for her. If she is not admitted to the United States, I shall go back with her. God willing, perhaps we can try again in a few years." There were many tears and hugs as the friends said good-bye.

"Yossel, we will work hard here," Yankel said. "When we will have saved enough money, we will send for our parents and also for you and Shifra. That is what friends are for."

Yankel and Shmuel were being sent to a village near Memphis, Tennessee. "What will we do there?" they asked the agent who was filling out their work papers.

"There is a new railroad line being built in that area," he replied. "You are young and have strong arms. Your job will be to dig earth and make railroad beds to lay the rail ties."

When the two friends arrived in the village, they found men working very hard, knee-deep in water.

"How is it here?" they asked a workman.

"We are like slaves," the workman whispered. "All we get is our food."

"Then we will run away," Yankel said under his breath. "We came here to work for a wage, not to be treated like slaves."

The construction foreman had overheard them. "Don't try to run away," he said. "You signed an agreement with the agent who paid your railroad fare to get you here. You are indebted to us. If I catch you trying to escape, my gun is sure to stop you."

After a few days of very difficult work, no sleep, and poor food, Yankel and Shmuel knew they had to escape.

When the foreman went into town to get supplies, Yankel and Shmuel fled. At nightfall, they knocked on a farmhouse door. They were hungry and needed a place to sleep. A black family lived there. "Would you have a place to sleep and some food?" Yankel used hand motions and a few English words to make himself understood. The family was kind to them and gave them bread and onions.

The next day, the man of the family took them to the nearest town, where they met a fellow Jew who gave them each some money and told them to go to Memphis. There they found work in a grocery store.

"Thank God for saving us from evil hands," Yankel later wrote to his parents. "If we work hard, it will not be long before we can send for you and Shmuel's parents, and also bring Yossel and Shifra back to America."

Lillian Wald

Lillian Wald.

How do you think you would feel if your parents told you that you were about to meet a distant relative for the first time? Perhaps you would feel excited, curious, and shy, all at the same time. But if your relative wore tattered clothes, spoke a different language, and needed help, you might want to forget about the meeting. On the other hand, you might say to yourself, "This is my relative. I have a responsibility to help this person."

The German Jews reacted in both these ways when they first met the Eastern European Jews who were arriving in the United States. Some of them were upset and didn't want to have much to do with the new immigrants, while many others practiced the Jewish concept of *hachnasat orechim,* "the welcoming of guests," the best way they could.

Lillian Wald, a daughter of a wealthy German Jewish family, was born in Cincinnati, Ohio, in 1867. Instead of spending her days attending parties as so many young people of her age did, she chose to help Jews in need. She studied nursing and began a nursing class on New York's Lower East Side.

Her goal was to help immigrant mothers improve the health of their families. She showed them how to keep their small apartments clean. She taught them about nutrition. She took food, medicine, and clean clothing to her patients in the tenements.

She also began a visiting nurses association. She demanded higher wages for immigrant workers and playgrounds for their children. She fought against child labor and for laws that eventually ended it. In addition, Miss Wald organized the Henry Street Settlement, which has continued her work of helping immigrants adjust to the United States. Lillian Wald was called "the angel of Henry Street" by the many people she helped. She died on September 1, 1940.

From the Writings of Lillian Wald

. . . Visit to 7 Hester Street . . . found two children with measles. After much argument, succeeded in bathing the two patients and the sick baby. . . . They [the parents] insisted no water and soap could be applied to anyone with measles before seven days. Brought clean dresses to the older children.

. . . Mrs. S. and [her] five children . . . five of the seven children are nearly naked. I am convinced that they have no apparel. Visited . . . family and rooms, and an effort is really being made to keep them and the children cleaner.

103

LABOR

When they first arrived in the United States in the early 1800s, East European Jewish immigrants had a difficult time. The average person worked in poor conditions for little pay. Factories and sweatshops were dreadful places. Germs spread fast in the airless rooms, and many of the workers became ill. When illness struck, the workers had no medical insurance.

In the 1860s, a few people began to organize themselves into unions. Unionizing became popular in the early 1900s as Jews and other immigrants became more and more determined to improve their poor working conditions.

The Triangle Shirtwaist Company.

The Rise of Labor Unions

The American Federation of Labor (AFL) was organized in 1886 by Samuel Gompers, an English-born Jew. In 1900, Jews living in New York formed the International Ladies Garment Workers Union (ILGWU). David Dubinsky served as its president from 1932 to 1966. In Chicago, Sidney Hillman, a former rabbinical student from Lithuania, became a labor organizer and helped found the Amalgamated Clothing Workers of America.

The unions fought for the rights of the workers. Sometimes, the workers went on strike. During the strike of 1910, thousands of people marched in the streets. They stayed away from their jobs for months and received no pay. They demanded that the unions be recognized by the factory owners. They wanted the owners to improve the working conditions in the factories.

The Triangle Fire

On March 25, 1911, a terrible tragedy occurred. A fire broke out in a factory occupied by the Triangle Shirtwaist Company in New York City. Hundreds of sewing-machine operators, mostly Jewish and Italian women, were working on the upper three floors of the company's ten-floor building when the fire broke out. They tried to escape, but the doors were locked because the bosses wanted to make sure that their workers didn't leave without permission. One hundred and forty-six people died in the fire. Factory owners could no longer ignore the cry to improve the poor working conditions.

As the unions became stronger, they helped the workers get many benefits, including health insurance and pensions. Unions also improved people's lives by organizing classes, concerts, and social events.

LABOR HEROES

Louis Dembitz Brandeis

Americans who were concerned about the poor working conditions of laborers had a

Supreme Court Justices Oliver Wendell Holmes and Louis D. Brandeis.

champion on their side. His name was Louis Dembitz Brandeis. The youngest of four children, Louis D. Brandeis was born in 1856 in Louisville, Kentucky.

Brandeis was a bright, serious student. Educated at Harvard Law School, he practiced law in Boston, Massachusetts. During his years in Boston, Brandeis spoke out against the terrible working conditions in factories. In 1910, he won rights for garment workers who had gone out on strike.

In his early years, Brandeis was not interested in his Jewish heritage. But he later came to believe strongly in the need for a Jewish homeland in Palestine. He was honorary president of the Zionist Organization of America.

In 1916, President Woodrow Wilson made Louis D. Brandeis a justice of the Supreme Court. He was the first Jew to be appointed to our nation's highest court. Today, Brandeis University and Brandeis Institute are named for him.

Rose Schneiderman

Rose Schneiderman.

In the early 1900s, a politician remarked that if women gained the right to vote, they would lose their beauty and charm. When Rose Schneiderman, a Jewish labor leader, heard this remark, she replied, "Women work in laundries and plants for thirteen to fourteen hours a day. Surely women won't lose any more of their beauty and charm by putting a ballot in a ballot box once a year than they are likely to lose standing in foundries and laundries all year round."

Rose Schneiderman was a determined woman. She was born in Poland in 1882 and

had come to the United States at the age of eight. Her father died when she was ten years old. By the time she was thirteen, she was working in a factory, making clothes. Her salary was $2.75 a week.

Rose was a born leader. Because the salaries and conditions of working women were dreadful, she decided to become a union organizer. She helped organize the International Ladies Garment Workers Union (ILGWU). For twenty-four years, she was president of the Women's Trade Union League. She served as secretary of the New York Department

of Labor and was a member of Franklin Roosevelt's Labor Advisory Board. The huge factory strikes that took place from 1909 to 1913 owed much of their success to this outspoken woman, who died in 1972.

IN THEIR OWN WORDS

The *Jewish Daily Forward*

The Yiddish language gave the Jewish immigrants a sense of community. On the Lower East Side in New York City, there were many Yiddish newspapers. One of the most popular features was a column in the *Jewish Daily Forward* that printed letters from readers. The column was called "Bintel Brief," which means "Bundle of Letters." After you read the letters below, make believe that you are the editor of the column and write an answer to one of them.

1906

Esteemed Editor,

When I arrived in New York, I walked around for two weeks looking for a job. . . . In the third week, I was lucky and found a job at which I earn eight dollars a week. I worked, I paid my landlady board, I bought a few things to wear, and I have a few dollars in my pocket.

Now I want you to advise me what to do. Should I send my father a few dollars for Passover, or should I keep the little money for myself? In this place, the work will end soon, and I may be left without a job.

1907

. . . there are seven people in our family. I am the oldest child, a fourteen-year-old girl. We have been in the country two years and my father, who is a frail man, is the only one working to support the whole family.

I go to school, where I do very well . . . but my father earned only $5.00 this week. I began to talk about giving up my studies and going to work in order to help my father as much as possible. My mother didn't even want to hear of it. She wants me to continue my education.

My mother is now pregnant, but she still has to take care of the three boarders we have in the house. Mother and Father work very hard, and they want to keep me in school. I beg you to tell me how to act.

Fill in the blanks.

The Russian czars forced the Jews to live in an area called the _____
_____. When Czar _____was assassinated, the peasants
took their anger out on the Jews. Some peasants attacked the Jews. These attacks
were called _____. The Russian government forced many Jewish boys
to _____.

Jews from Russia began to immigrate to the United States in the late 1800s. _____
_____ and _____were two ports of entry. Almost two and
a half million Jews came to America, but in the year _____, Congress passed
laws that _____
_____.

Most of the immigrants settled on the _____ of New
York City. They spoke the _____ language. Many worked in the needle
trade in airless rooms called _____. After work, immigrants went to the
_____, where they read books and newspapers in order to learn English. Religious schools called _____were poorly run. Soon, however,
_____, with their more modern curriculum, replaced these schools.

DISCUSSION

1. The immigration policies of countries still make news. Do you think that the United
States should admit anyone who wants to immigrate to this country?

2. Our government now passes special measures allowing some people who are experiencing political and religious problems in their homeland to immigrate. Do you
know a recent immigrant? Discuss the difficulties of settling in a new country.

ACTIVITIES

1. On a world map, put flags on the countries from which your family came. Make a table of statistics that shows the number of family members who came from each country.

2. Write an imaginary scene between an immigrant and an immigration official in the early 1900s.

3. Start an immigration museum in your school. Ask people who came from another country to lend you something they brought with them. The item may be a photograph, a letter, a religious object, a passport, a birth certificate, etc. Label each item, showing the year and country of its origin.

4. Write your own "Bintel Brief." Exchange letters with a classmate, and answer his or her letter. Share your letter and answer with the class.

5. In the early 1900s, immigrant children your age often had to work instead of going to school. Interview an older person who came to the United States as a child in order to find out about that person's schooling and when he or she began to work.

CHAPTER 10

SEPHARDIM IN AMERICA

LINKS IN HISTORY

The Collapse of the Ottoman Empire

You have been reading about immigrants who came to the United States first from Western Europe and then from Central Europe.

In the early 1900s, thousands of immigrants also came to these shores from other countries. War, poverty, and the desire for a better life all contributed to large immigrations from countries in Asia and from a group of lands in Eastern Europe known as the Balkans.

In this chapter, you will learn about Jewish immigration from Turkish lands and from the Balkans. In order to fully understand this wave of Jewish immigration, you must know something about the countries from which these people came.

The Ottoman Empire consisted of lands

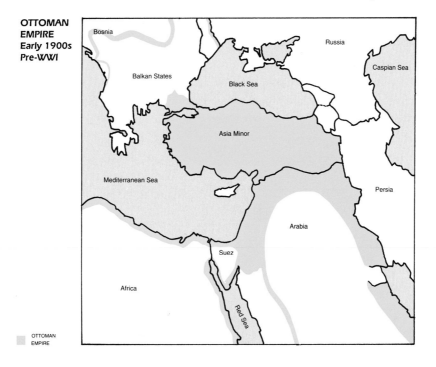

OTTOMAN EMPIRE
Early 1900s
Pre-WWI

Bosnia
Russia
Balkan States
Black Sea
Caspian Sea
Asia Minor
Mediterranean Sea
Persia
Arabia
Suez
Africa
Red Sea

OTTOMAN EMPIRE

ruled by the Turks. It was named for a Turkish ruler, Osman I, who lived in the Middle Ages. Part of this empire was on the continent of Europe, and part of it was in Asia. For hundreds of years, the Ottoman Turks controlled Greece, portions of Asia, the islands in the Aegean Sea, and the Balkans.

Today, the Balkans, bounded by the Adriatic, Aegean, and Black seas, consist of present-day Albania, Bulgaria, Greece, Romania, and the republics of what was formerly Yugoslavia. The boundaries and rulers of these countries have changed frequently.

In 1908, a revolt, known as the Young Turks Rebellion, broke out in Turkey. In 1913, the Balkans defeated Turkey and regained control of their lands. When the United States entered World War I in 1917, the Ottoman Empire was no longer a strong power. It came to an end in 1918 when Germany, its ally, lost the war.

THE JEWISH EXPERIENCE

Until the mid-1700s, most of the Jews in the United States were of Sephardic origin. In the early chapters of this book, you read that the Jews of Spain and Portugal went to Holland, Central and South America, the Caribbean Islands, and the American colonies after their expulsion in 1492.

THE TWENTIETH CENTURY Along with the vast number of Ashkenazic Jews who came to the United States during the first quarter of the 1900s, a smaller group of Sephardim also immigrated to the United States. These were Jews whose ancestors had traveled east and south of Spain and Portugal to lands in the Balkans, Asia, and North Africa. In the twentieth century, many of them immigrated to America from Turkey; Salonika, a city in Greece; Rhodes, an island in the Aegean Sea; Aleppo, a city in Syria; and North Africa.

Among the first Sephardim to arrive in the twentieth century were tradesmen who came to sell their Oriental rugs and Turkish cigarettes at the St. Louis World's Fair in 1904. Many of them stayed and established American branches of their businesses.

Early in the twentieth century, as a result of the rebellion in Turkey in 1908 and the war in the Balkans in 1912 to 1913, thousands of Jews fled to the United States from these countries. After World War II, people from the Balkans who had survived the Holocaust came to these shores. More recently, in the 1950s and 1960s, Sephardim from Iraq, Egypt, North Africa, and Iran have made their home here. The latest group to arrive are Sephardim from Israel. The exact number of Sephardim in the United States today is not certain, but is said to be about one hundred and fifty thousand and growing.

IN AMERICA When they first arrived in the United States, the Sephardim, like all other Jewish immigrants, faced many

Sephardic Jews posed for this photograph at the 1904 St. Louis World's Fair.

Iranian Jews are part of the mosaic that is America.

hardships. They had to find a way to make a living. Because they had strong family ties, their first goal was to send money back home and bring other members of their family to America.

HIAS, the Hebrew Immigrant Aid Society, tried to help the Sephardim when they first arrived at Ellis Island. Many times, however, the organization did not make contact with these Jews because HIAS officials were unfamiliar with Sephardic names and did not recognize them as being Jewish.

La America, a leading Judeo-Spanish newspaper, was established in 1910 by Moses Gadol, a successful Sephardic businessman who had come from Bulgaria. He urged the Sephardim to become citizens, learn English, and acquaint themselves with American ways. Another Judeo-Spanish publication, the weekly *La Vara*, also taught the Sephardim about American customs.

Congregation Shearith Israel, the oldest Spanish Portuguese synagogue in New York City, established many programs to help the new immigrants. It organized and supported a synagogue on the Lower East Side for the new arrivals. The sisterhood of Congregation Shearith Israel ran a settlement house to teach the Sephardic immigrants the skills that they needed in order to adapt to American life.

The new immigrants also helped one another. They met in Turkish-style coffeehouses, where they traded information about the old country. They told one another about English classes, and they learned of job opportunities. As soon as

New York's Congregation Shearith Israel, also known as the Spanish and Portuguese Synagogue, originated as the synagogue on Mill Street in 1730.

they could, the immigrants began to form groups that worked for the benefit of the community. Today, there are organizations such as the American Sephardi Federation, Sephardic Jewish Brotherhood of America, and the Union of Sephardic Congregations.

Benjamin Nathan Cardozo

Supreme Court Justice Benjamin Nathan Cardozo.

Someday, you may be asked to name a person whose life is an example of the best that American and Jewish culture has produced. If you answer Benjamin Nathan Cardozo, you will have made a fine choice.

Benjamin Cardozo was born into an old American Sephardic family in the year 1870. The family traces its roots all the way back to Gershom Mendes Seixas, who was the patriotic leader of Congregation Shearith Israel during the American Revolution.

Chazan Seixas was Benjamin's great-granduncle. Benjamin's father, Albert, was a justice of the Supreme Court of New York.

The Cardozo home was spacious and happy. Ben had many siblings and cousins with whom to play. But tragedy struck when Ben was nine years old. First, his mother died. Then, his father was accused of using his position as a judge to help certain politicians unlawfully. Albert Cardozo had to resign in disgrace from the court. He died when Ben was a teenager. Ben was raised by his older sister Nellie, who devoted her life to her brother. Neither Ben nor Nellie ever married.

Benjamin Cardozo was an honor student at Columbia University, where he studied law. He was elected justice of the Supreme Court of New York and later became the chief judge of the Court of Appeals, the highest court of the state. In 1932, President Herbert Hoover appointed Benjamin Cardozo justice of the Supreme Court of the United States, a position he held for six years.

Benjamin Cardozo was a devoted Jew his whole life. He was a member of Congregation Shearith Israel in New York City. He was the guest speaker for many Jewish organizations. Before he died in 1938, he asked that his funeral be simple. The traditional prayers and chants of the Sephardic prayer book were recited in Hebrew at his grave.

The Jewish Fishermen

In 1903, two Jews, Solomon Calvo and Jacob Policar, immigrated to Seattle, Washington, from the Turkish island of Marmara, in the Sea of Marmara. They were the first of many Sephardim to go to Seattle.

It is hard for us to imagine their trip.

They traveled across the Mediterranean Sea, crossed the Atlantic Ocean, and took a train over the 3,000-mile expanse of the United States. Solomon and Jacob were accompanied on their trip by a Greek friend, Alexi.

"Wake up, Solomon! Wake up, Jacob!" Alexi said in Greek, as he woke his friends from an uncomfortable sleep. The three had been traveling and sleeping on trains from New York City for over a week. "Jacob, Solomon," Alexi continued, "we're here. We are finally in Seattle. Our trip is over."

The three men hired a large wagon and a horse to carry their belongings to the fish market that Alexi owned near the waterfront area. Jacob and Solomon had each brought many bags with them, since they were immigrating to America. Whatever they thought they might need for their new life had been carefully packed in Marmara.

Alexi, a Greek school friend who had immigrated to Seattle a few years before, had returned to the island of Marmara to visit his parents. He had persuaded his two friends to go back to Seattle with him. The other Jews in Marmara had not been encouraging. "Seattle? Where is Seattle? What will you do there? Are there any other Jews there?" they asked. To them, going

The Seattle seaport at the turn of the twentieth century.

to Seattle was like going to the end of the earth.

Alexi, who was not Jewish, told them that there was plenty of work in Seattle, much like the work that they did in Marmara. Each day, the men of Marmara went out to fish. Some people made a living by cleaning and packing the fish for shipment to other places. Alexi told them that Seattle was a town near the Pacific Ocean and that people there also made a living from fish. He offered to house anyone who wanted to go to Seattle. Alexi also said that he had customers who were Jewish, although he didn't know anything about these Jews.

Soon Jacob, Solomon, and Alexi arrived at the fish market. The room in the back of the market was old and shabby, but at least it was a place to sleep. Jacob and Solomon looked around the neighborhood with appreciative eyes. There were many fish stalls and other small food stores. The street was filled with people. The newcomers could see the busy harbor just down the street, where people were hard at work unloading the daily catch. The ocean breeze and the smell of the fish reminded Jacob and Solomon of Marmara.

The next day, Alexi put them to work in the market. Toward noon, two customers came into the store to buy fish. Alexi spoke to the men in English and brought them over to meet Jacob and Solomon.

With big smiles on their faces, the customers shook hands with the newcomers and said, *"Shalom Alechem, fun velcha shtat kumst du?"*

Jacob turned to Solomon and said in Ladino, "I think I heard them say *Shalom Alechem*, which is a Jewish greeting. But what else are they saying?"

Alexi, seeing the puzzled look on his friends' faces, said to them in Greek, "These men are Jews. Don't you understand their language?"

Solomon answered, "Please ask them what language they are speaking. Tell them that we speak Ladino, which is a combination of Spanish, Hebrew, and Greek."

When Alexi relayed this information to the men, they began to shake their heads. Alexi seemed to be trying to convince them about something.

It was now Alexi's turn to be puzzled. "They say that they spoke to you in Yiddish, the language of the Jews in Europe. They have never heard of Ladino. Furthermore, they think that you can't possibly be Jews since you are in the fish business. They have never heard of Jewish fishermen."

"Tell them that I can convince them that we are Jews," said Solomon. He ran to the room in the back of the market and came back holding a Hebrew prayer book and a *talit*. "Here," he practically shouted at the men in Ladino, "here is a *siddur* and here is a *talit*."

The men looked at the book and then examined the *talit*. *"Leyen die tefilah,"* one of them said, pointing to a sentence in the book.

The word *tefilah* sounded familiar to the young men because it is Hebrew for "prayer." Both Jacob and Solomon looked at the sentence that the man was pointing to and recited together, *"Shema Yisrael, Adonai Elohenu, Adonai Echad."*

The men's faces relaxed into broad smiles as they grabbed the hands of the two young fishermen. *"Shalom Alechem,"* they exclaimed, hugging the newcomers. *"Du zeinen take Yidden."* ("You are really Jews.")

SEPHARDIC CUSTOMS

Imagine the following scene, which might have taken place during the 1920s. A young woman brings a young man home for her mama and papa to meet. Mama and Papa are very polite but a little uneasy. The young man is different from the Jews that they are used to. His skin tone is more olive, and he speaks English with an accent that they have not heard before. They ask the young man where he is from.

"Rhodes," he replies.

Mama and Papa look at each other in bewilderment. "Your accent is strange to us. What language do you speak at home?" they ask.

"My family speaks Ladino, but we also speak Greek," the young man answers.

By this time, the girl's parents are very uncomfortable. For one thing, they have no idea what Ladino is, and they are not quite sure where Rhodes is in relation to their native Poland.

Finally, Mama blurts out the question that is really on her mind. "Are you Jewish?" Mama asks.

This time, the young woman answers. "Of course, he's Jewish, Mama. But he is not Ashkenazic like us. He is Sephardic."

Now imagine the following scene. The Sephardic young man has taken the Ashkenazic young woman home to meet his parents. It is Rosh Hashanah, and there is a large family gathering around the table for dinner. At the head of the table sits the grandfather. He is dressed in a beautifully embroidered robe. Before the family

eats, the grandfather blesses all of the children.

Then the food is brought in from the kitchen. There is fish with a lemon and egg sauce, an eggplant salad, and vegetables, including okra and leeks. There is couscous, bourekas, olives, and, for dessert, baklava and marzipan. The young man's mama and papa already know that the young woman is Jewish, but they are just as uneasy as her parents were.

"This fish is delicious," the

(continued)

young woman says. "I have never had anything like it before."

When the couscous is served, the young woman is puzzled. "What kind of grain is this?" she asks.

Instead of answering, the young man's brother asks, "What kind of fish do you eat on this holiday?"

"Gefilte fish," the young woman answers.

Everyone is too polite to ask what gefilte fish is. Instead, someone asks, "If you don't eat couscous, what do you eat?"

"My mama often makes kasha," she replies.

Before anyone can ask "What's kasha?" Grandfather clears his throat and begins to talk about the holiday.

Mama takes the young woman into the kitchen and explains the different foods to her. Then she says what is on her mind.

"Our customs are different. Do you think that you could learn about our foods and cook them for our son when you are married?"

"I think I could," replies the young woman. "In our household, we intend to observe both Ashkenazic and Sephardic customs."

When you read the above story, you also may have found yourself asking about some of the Sephardic *minhagim*, or "customs." The language that many Sephardim speak is **Ladino**, or Judeo-Spanish. Ladino is a mixture of Spanish, Hebrew, and the language of the countries in which various Sephardic groups settled.

Sephardim have very close-knit families and often settle together in a community. They also like to settle among people who emigrated from the same towns in Europe and Asia as they did. However, since the 1920s, it has become common for the children of Sephardim to marry the children of Ashkenazim.

Sephardim have great respect for their older family members. One lovely custom that they observe occurs when a parent or a grandparent is called to recite the blessings over the Torah or to read the Torah portion during the synagogue service. The younger relatives stand and remain standing until the elder is finished. When the father or grandfather leaves the *bimah,* the children line up to kiss his hand. In return, they receive his blessing.

Sephardim name their children after living relatives. They believe that by doing this, they provide their children with a living role model.

The foods that Sephardim eat are popular in the lands from which they came. On Passover, some Sephardim eat peas, beans, and rice. These foods are not eaten by Ashkenazim on this holiday.

Today, some customs that originated with the Sephardim are observed by most Jews in the United States. For instance, the music in many synagogues includes well-known Sephardic melodies. Some of the *piyutim,* or religious poems of Sephardic origin, are a part of every synagogue prayer book. Even modern Hebrew is spoken according to the Sephardic pronunciation.

Reread the chapter and fill in the missing information.

1. Name some of the Balkan countries. _____
   _____
   _____

2. The _____ Empire was ruled by the Turks.

3. Sephardim are Jews who originally came from _____ and
   _____ .

4. The main groups of Sephardim in the United States come from
   a. _____   b. _____
   c. _____   d. _____ .

5. As a result of the war in the _____ in 1912 to 1913, thousands
   of Sephardim immigrated to the United States.

6. Two early Sephardic newspapers were _____
   _____ .

7. The language spoken by Sephardim from Turkey and Greece is _____ .

8. _____ , a gentleman of Sephardic origin, was a
   brilliant justice of the Supreme Court.

9. The Hebrew word for *customs* is _____ .

10. _____ is a grain eaten by many Sephardim.

DISCUSSION

Do you think that it takes courage to leave your family and friends and go to live in a faraway place? Would you be willing to do this?

ACTIVITIES

1. Learn more about Sephardic *minhagim*. If you live in a community that has a Sephardic population, invite the rabbi or a member of the Sephardic synagogue to your school to discuss Sephardic customs. Make a chart showing Ashkenazic and Sephardic *minhagim* for Shabbat, bar and bat mitzvah, holidays, etc.

	ASHKENAZIC	SEPHARDIC
Shabbat		
Bar and bat mitzvah		
High Holidays		
Other holidays		

2. Israelis of Sephardic origin, Iranian Jews, and Moroccan Jews are the most recent Sephardic groups to immigrate to North America. Conduct a survey to identify all of the countries of origin of Jews who have arrived in your community during the last ten years. Make posters highlighting the countries from which they came. Add photographs to the posters. Display Jewish ceremonial objects that these groups use in their home on holidays and special occasions.

3. The customs of Sephardic and Ashkenazic Jews may be different, but both groups share many of the same ideas and beliefs. Write an essay about how Jewish ideas and beliefs have kept us together as one people.

4. On white paper plates, draw and color a typical Ashkenazic and Sephardic holiday meal. Perhaps you and your classmates can cook an Ashkenazic and a Sephardic meal for a Shabbat celebration.

CHAPTER 11

AMERICAN JUDAISM

LINKS IN HISTORY

Many Ways to Express Ourselves

Many changes in the way Americans lived took place in the years before and after World War I. New inventions began to change everyday life. Things we take for granted today, such as automobiles, radios, and telephones, became part of American culture. Highways were built, and more people were able to buy their own homes.

At that time, many people believed that America should be a **melting pot**. According to this idea, immigrants should let go of their ties to the countries from which they had come. The ideal was for immigrants to assimilate into American culture and give up their native languages and customs. But many immigrants had another idea: They wanted to hold onto their traditional customs and make these customs part of their life in America. They felt that America should promote the different ethnic, racial, and religious groups that were becoming part of the mosaic of life in America. This idea is called **pluralism**.

THE JEWISH EXPERIENCE

Jewish immigrants came from many backgrounds. They spoke different languages, read different newspapers, and ate different foods. Jewish leaders wanted to make the Jewish community strong and also help the newcomers fit into American society. They developed various plans and organizations to accomplish these goals.

JEWISH UNITY In large cities such as New York, the need arose for an organization that would unify all Jews. Judah Leib Magnes, an American-born Reform rabbi, worked especially hard to bring unity to the different groups in New York City. In 1908, he established an organization called the **Kehillah**. The Kehillah

The Hester Street market was the heart of New York's Lower East Side. This photograph, taken by Jacob Riis, shows a typical business day.

promoted Jewish education, fought crime, and helped the various Jewish groups work together. In 1922, Rabbi Magnes, a committed Zionist, left his duties at the Kehillah and emigrated to Palestine where, in 1925, he founded the Hebrew University in Jerusalem.

One of the projects of the Kehillah was the Bureau of Jewish Education, which helped provide a Jewish education for Jewish children in New York City. Samson Benderly, an educator of Sephardic origin who was born in Safed, Palestine, was the leader of the Bureau of Jewish Education between 1910 and 1920. Today, bureaus of

Jewish education work with religious schools in many American cities.

JEWISH RIGHTS Two organizations spoke out for Jewish rights during this period. The American Jewish Committee was organized in 1906, and the American Jewish Congress was formed in 1917. During the peace conference that ended World War I, the American Jewish Congress sent delegates to represent the Jewish communities in Europe. They tried to make the peacemakers aware of the desperate need for a Jewish homeland in Palestine.

Another organization, the American

Jewish Joint Distribution Committee (JDC), collected millions of dollars to provide relief for Jewish victims during and after the war. In addition, the JDC shipped food and medical supplies to Jews living in Palestine. Yet another organization, the Jewish Welfare Board, helped American Jewish soldiers fighting in foreign lands.

NEXT YEAR IN JERUSALEM While hundreds of thousands of Jews were immigrating to America in the late 1800s and early 1900s, other Jews were dreaming of the land of Israel.

Palestine, the Roman name for Israel, had not been a Jewish country for almost eighteen hundred years, although Jews had always lived there. This land had been conquered by many people over the centuries. In the 1800s, Turkey ruled the region.

Jews continued to hope that one day they would be able to return to the land promised to them in the Bible. In the late 1800s, a movement started, calling for a return to Zion and the reestablishment of a Jewish community in Palestine. We call this movement **Zionism**.

As persecution increased in Russia in the 1890s, young Jews found their way to Palestine, where they set up agricultural colonies. Life was very difficult for these early pioneers. The Turkish government

The first Jewish pioneers in Palestine were called *chalutzim*.

did not encourage the newcomers. Malaria, a deadly disease spread by mosquitoes, was everywhere. However, the *chalutzim*, or "pioneers," were determined to succeed.

No one worked harder for the Zionist dream than Theodor Herzl, a journalist from Vienna, Austria. Herzl invited Jewish leaders to meet in Basle, Switzerland, in 1897. The goal of this meeting, known as the **First Zionist Congress**, was to call for the establishment of a Jewish homeland in Palestine.

AMERICAN ZIONISM Many Jewish citizens of the United States began to organize Zionist groups and work for this goal. However, there were numerous debates about this issue. Some felt that the Jewish people were not a nation but a religious community. These people maintained that Jews were meant to spread the message of the Bible to all people. In order to fulfill this mission, Jews were destined to live in many countries. Some people argued that an American could not be a loyal citizen if he or she supported another country.

Other Jews, particularly many of the recent immigrants, disagreed. For them, Palestine was the rightful home of the Jewish people, promised to them in the Bible. These people believed that Jews would never gain the respect of the world if they continued to be a people without a land. They maintained that Jews could be both loyal American citizens and loyal Zionists. You have already read how Louis D. Brandeis set an example for American Jews by becoming president of the Zionist Organization of America.

During World War I, Turkey was an ally of Germany and still ruled Palestine. In 1917, the British government issued a paper known as the **Balfour Declaration**. It said that the government of Great Britain was in favor of a Jewish state in Palestine. After the war, Palestine became a part of the British Empire.

The Jews of America rejoiced when they read Britain's declaration. They sent delegates to the peace conference that ended World War I at Versailles, France, to represent the Zionist cause. Among the representatives was a young rabbi, Stephen S. Wise, who was to become a great American Jewish leader.

Those who had argued that Jews could continue to be good citizens of the United States as well as Zionists proved to be right. They helped show that it was possible for Jews to be productive citizens of one country and still support their fellow Jews in another.

TRADITIONAL JUDAISM America presented the Jewish immigrants with many new challenges. How to help people observe traditional Judaism in a land in which there was so much freedom posed a major challenge to Jewish leaders.

In the small towns of Europe, families had found comfort and security in being close to one another. Life revolved around the Sabbath and Jewish holidays. In America, Jewish fathers and mothers were often too busy trying to support their families to practice religious observances. In their desire to become Americanized as quickly as possible, young Jews often embraced ideas that were different from those of their parents. They viewed the *shul*s in which their parents prayed as being part of the old country. Some of them turned away from Judaism altogether. Others searched for ways to make the synagogue more meaningful to life in America.

Reform Judaism, which had developed many years before, was a solution for some. However, the immigrants of the late 1800s and early 1900s often did not feel comfortable in the well-established Reform temples. Jewish leaders of that time realized that a need for a traditional yet modern synagogue existed. They wanted a synagogue in which Hebrew would be used in the service, but English would be used for sermons and lessons. They wanted to preserve the joy of worship that existed in the *shul*s of Eastern Europe. But they also admired the orderliness of the services in the great Ashkenazic and Sephardic synagogues of Germany, England, and Holland.

CONSERVATIVE JUDAISM Two Sephardic leaders, Dr. Sabato Morais, the Italian-born Sephardic *chazan* of Congregation Mikveh Israel in Philadelphia, and Rabbi Henry Pereira Mendes of Congregation Shearith Israel in New York, as well as the scholarly Rabbi Alexander Kohut from Hungary, founded the **Jewish Theological Seminary of America** in 1886. Its purpose was to train traditional American rabbis.

In organizing the seminary, they were following the path of Rabbi Zacharias Frankel, who had founded a similar school in Breslau, Germany. Frankel believed that Jews not only experienced God and Torah at Mount Sinai but also have an ongoing experience with God that permits them to change the practice of Judaism.

In America, these ideas came to be known as Conservative Judaism. The faculty of the Jewish Theological Seminary consisted of scholars from both Sephardic

Dr. Sabato Morais, a founder of the Jewish Theological Seminary.

Dr. Solomon Schechter, the first president of the Jewish Theological Seminary.

125

and Ashkenazic backgrounds. Besides Sabato Morais, it included such scholars as Marcus Jastrow, Alexander Kohut, Henry Pereira Mendes, Bernard Drachman, and Frederick de Sola Mendes. In 1902, after the death of both Dr. Morais and Rabbi Kohut, the seminary made Dr. Solomon Schechter, a famous professor from Cambridge University in England, its president. He brought great Jewish scholars from Europe to the seminary and helped it grow into an important center of Jewish learning.

In 1913, many synagogues got together and formed a federation known as the **United Synagogue of America**. This organization represents Conservative synagogues to this day.

THE ORTHODOX MOVEMENT Although the Conservative movement met the needs of many immigrants, there were some who felt that it had made too many changes. These Jews, known as Orthodox Jews, believe that *halachah*—the laws of Judaism—and Jewish traditions should be strictly followed and not altered.

In the late 1800s, those who wanted to maintain traditional Judaism and not make any changes in Jewish law felt that they could do this only if they were unified under a great rabbi. In 1888, Rabbi Jacob Joseph, a respected rabbi from Vilna, Lithuania, was invited to become the chief rabbi of New York.

The position of chief rabbi was common in European countries. The chief rabbi's duties were to see that the community's food was kosher, that its cemeteries were maintained, and that the customs of its synagogues did not differ too much from one another.

Fifteen synagogues in New York City joined to bring Rabbi Jacob Joseph from Vilna to lead them. At first, he had a loyal following. After a short time, however, some people began to question why one rabbi should have authority over all other rabbis. The idea of having a chief rabbi did not work in the United States. Under the leadership of Congregation Shearith Israel, the original Spanish Portuguese synagogue in New York, the **Union of Orthodox Jewish Congregations** was formed to represent Orthodox Jews.

Jewish education is very important to Orthodox Jews. At first, they organized afternoon Hebrew schools. Later on, they established day schools called *yeshivot* as an alternative to public education. Both

Rabbi Jacob Joseph was appointed chief rabbi of New York City in 1888.

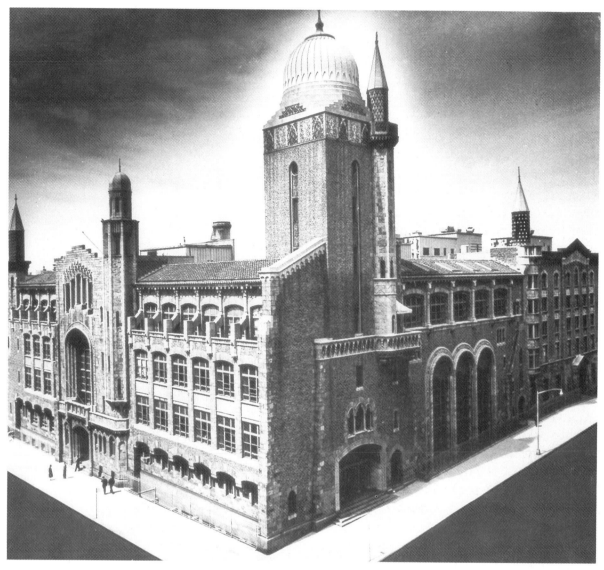

Yeshiva University.

Hebrew and English subjects are taught in *yeshivot*. Since the 1950s, *yeshivot* have become very popular among Orthodox Jews. Conservative and Reform Jews have also established day schools in many major cities.

Two schools for the advanced study of the Talmud and other Jewish religious texts were established in New York, one in 1886 and the other in 1897. By 1928, under the leadership of Rabbi Bernard Revel, these schools became Yeshiva College. In 1945, the college became **Yeshiva University**. Today, the university, which includes the Albert Einstein College of Medicine and the Cardozo School of Law, is world famous.

No Thunder Sounded, No Lightning Struck
by Judith Kaplan Eisenstein

In the 1920s, as people debated what Judaism meant and how to keep it alive in America, one man, Mordecai Kaplan, a rabbi and teacher at the Jewish Theological Seminary, went one step farther than anyone had before. He claimed that Judaism is more than just a religion or a nationality—it is a great civilization. A civilization includes music, art, science, and advanced ways of living together. Dr. Kaplan believed that American Jews live in two civilizations—Jewish civilization and American civilization. He spoke and wrote about his idea, developing it into a new movement in Judaism called **Reconstuctionism**. *The word* reconstruct *means to "build again."*

In 1922, Dr. Kaplan founded the Society for the Advancement of Judaism. Its synagogue had meeting rooms, a dining room, and a gymnasium so as to encourage Jews to come together not just to pray but also to study, eat, and exercise. Today, there are many Reconstructionist synagogues. Dr. Kaplan's ideas continue to influence synagogues and Jewish community centers throughout the United States.

Dr. Mordecai Kaplan, founder of the Reconstructionist movement.

Dr. Kaplan felt that women should have a more important role in the religious service. He was determined to do something about this situation. In the following story, Dr. Kaplan's daughter, Dr. Judith Kaplan Eisenstein, a famous educator, tells how she was a "guinea pig" for one of her father's ideas.

It was a sunny Friday afternoon in early May of 1922. My two grandmothers were gently rocking in the chairs that my father had bought for them. They were having an intense conversation in Yiddish. I was in my bedroom. I am certain that they did not want me to understand what they were saying. But I understand Yiddish, and since Grandma Rubin was slightly deaf, they spoke quite loudly. I heard every word.

"You are his mother," my mother's mother said. "Talk to your son. Tell him not to do this thing!"

"You know a son doesn't listen to his mother," Grandma Kaplan replied angrily. "You talk to your daughter. Tell her to tell him not to do this thing!"

I must say that I had very confused feelings as I listened to their conversation. My father was planning to present me as a bat mitzvah in the synagogue during Shabbat services the next morning. It would be the first bat mitzvah ever. I was both frightened by and excited about this event. I was also bewildered by my grandmothers' angry voices.

My father had first brought up the subject several months before. It was on my twelfth birthday, the age when a Jewish girl assumes the responsibility of doing *mitzvot*. "Judith," he had said that day, "you know how I feel about women having a more active role in the synagogue ritual."

"Yes, Father," I replied, wondering what this statement had to do with me.

"When the Society for the Advancement of Judaism moves into the synagogue that we have purchased, I will see to it that you have a bat mitzvah," my father went on.

"But Father, there is no such thing." I looked at him with a startled expression. "My girlfriends have had confirmations, but I have never heard of a bat mitzvah ceremony."

"Of course, you haven't heard of it," my father replied, giving me a hug. "That's because no such ceremony exists. But that does not mean that there shouldn't be one. As soon as the synagogue is ready, I will develop a ceremony for a bat mitzvah, and you, my dear child, will be the first one."

My grandmothers' uneasiness brought back the unsettled feelings that I had experienced when my father had first told me of his plan. Of course, I also felt that women should have a more active part in the ritual of the synagogue.

In addition to the synagogue service, my parents were having a big party at our home to celebrate the event on *motzaei Shabbat* (the "evening following the Sabbath"). I was very flattered that I was going to be the center of all of this attention, but I was also a little worried.

"What will my friends say?" I wondered. "I hope that they won't make fun of me." When you are twelve and a half, you think about things like that. After all, who wants to be different? Then, too, my father, who was so busy with the new synagogue, had not told me what I was going to do!

That evening, after our Shabbat dinner, my father took me into his study. "Judith," he said, "tomorrow you will read a portion of the *parashah* we call the Holiness Code."

"But Father, I do not know how to chant from the Torah." I could feel myself getting red in the face.

"Don't worry," my father said reassuringly. "Perhaps someday soon, women will chant from the *Sefer Torah* itself, but for now, what you will do is read from your *Chumash* after the Torah has been rolled and dressed in its mantle. Now let's practice the blessing that is said before and after the portion."

The next morning, we all went to the synagogue. My mother, my three little sisters, and my grandmothers sat in the back of the synagogue. Even though my father's ideas were considered advanced, our synagogue was traditional. Women sat apart from the men. But I had to sit up front

with the men, away from the protection of my mother and sisters.

The Torah was read. Then my father read the *maftir* (the concluding portion of the Torah) and the *haftarah* (the reading from the Prophets). Now it was my turn. I stood below the *bimah* because women were not allowed on the *bimah*, even in my father's synagogue. As I looked out at the congregation, I felt very anxious. I worried that I would forget how to read my portion. Would my parents be proud of me? Would the scowls on my grandmothers' faces turn to smiles? I read the blessing, and in a loud voice I read the selection my father had chosen for me, first in Hebrew and then in English.

That was it! The scroll was returned to the ark, and the service went on. Much to my grandmothers' amazement, no thunder sounded and no lightning struck. My girl-friends did not quite understand what all the fuss was about, but they did not tease me or think that I was odd. In fact, they had a wonderful time at my party.

Times have changed. My daughters, like most Jewish girls, have learned not only to read the Torah portion but to chant from the Torah scroll itself. Jewish girls not only take their bat mitzvahs for granted now, they can even become rabbis and cantors. I, however, will never forget that I was the very first bat mitzvah.

Stephen Samuel Wise

Stephen Samuel Wise was an American rabbi who knew many presidents. Born in Budapest, Hungary, in 1874, he immigrated with his family to the United States when he was a child. After he graduated with honors from Columbia University, he went to Vienna to study for the rabbinate.

Rabbi Wise loved the Jewish people. He wanted to see the Jews settled in their ancient homeland, Israel. He devoted his entire life to this goal. In order to be able to speak freely about Zionism and other Jewish issues, he founded the Free Synagogue in New York City.

After World War I, Rabbi Wise attended the Versailles Peace Conference, where he spoke on behalf of Jewish causes.

He traveled throughout the United States, telling people about his love for Israel. When Franklin Delano Roosevelt became president, Wise visited him many times. Each time, he spoke about his dream of a Jewish homeland. Rabbi Wise was a founder of the Federation of American Zionists, which later became the Zionist Organization of America (ZOA).

Stephen Wise worked not only for his own people but for all people who needed help. He was one of the founders of the National Association for the Advancement of Colored People (NAACP). He also founded the American Civil Liberties Union (ACLU),

Rabbi Stephen S. Wise *(center)* with Albert Einstein *(left)* and New York City Mayor Fiorello La Guardia *(right)*.

an organization that helps people who feel that they are being discriminated against.

Rabbi Wise worked hard for Jewish unity. In 1922, he established the Jewish Institute of Religion, a seminary that trained rabbis for all branches of Judaism. He hoped that rabbis from his school would be called upon to serve in any Jewish congregation, regardless of the ritual differences. Rabbi Wise died in 1949, one year after the establishment of the State of Israel. He lived to see the fulfillment of his life's work.

Henrietta Szold

Henrietta Szold, the eldest of the five daughters of Rabbi Benjamin Szold of Baltimore, Maryland, never married or had children of her own. However, she was a mother of the Jewish people.

Henrietta Szold was born in Baltimore in the year 1860. Her father believed that girls should receive as fine an education as boys did. As a result, Henrietta studied Hebrew, Bible, and Jewish history with him, in addition to her subjects at school. When she was quite young, she translated books from German into English.

To help poor immigrants from Eastern Europe who had settled in Baltimore, Henrietta Szold suggested that a night school be founded. She taught and supervised at the school. Educators heard of the school's great success and came from all over the country to learn about her methods.

In 1912, Miss Szold visited Palestine. At this time, Turkey ruled that country. Life there was difficult, and people were poor. Seeing that the basic needs of medicine and sanitation were not available to the Jews who lived there made Henrietta Szold very sad. Soon after her return to America, she organized Hadassah, the Women's Zionist Organization of America.

The first Hadassah mission in Palestine in 1920.

Henrietta Szold as a teenager.

Henrietta Szold dancing in Palestine with members of Youth Aliyah.

Very quickly, Hadassah began to provide relief to the Jews of Palestine. It sent nurses and medical supplies to fight dreaded diseases like malaria and trachoma. In time, as Hadassah's work expanded under Henrietta Szold's direction, a hospital and medical school were founded. Today, they are known as the Rothschild-Hadassah-University Hospital and Medical School in Jerusalem. Both Jews and Arabs go there to receive the finest medical treatment available.

But Henrietta Szold soon realized that her work was not completed. In 1933, Jews living in Germany were becoming victims of persecution. Miss Szold felt that she had to do everything in her power to rescue the children. As a result, she organized the Youth Aliyah movement. She and her friends worked to transport thousands of Jewish children to Palestine, where she established villages for them and supervised their education. When she died in 1945, Jews throughout the world mourned for this great leader.

Fill in the blanks with the correct names. Then choose one of the people listed below and research his or her life.

Henrietta Szold   Judah Leib Magnes
Sabato Morais   Mordecai Kaplan
Jacob Joseph   Stephen S. Wise
Judith Kaplan Eisenstein Solomon Schechter

1. A founder of the Jewish Theological Seminary._____

2. The founder of Hadassah._____

3. A founder of the Zionist Organization of America._____

4. The first bat mitzvah._____

5. The first president of the Hebrew University in Jerusalem._____

6. The Cambridge scholar who became the president of the Jewish Theological Seminary._____

7. The founder of Reconstructionism._____

8. The Orthodox leader who became New York's first and only chief rabbi._____

_____

DISCUSSION

1. Some people feel that the only true way to express their devotion to Israel is to live there. Other people feel that the best way to show their love for Israel is to donate money to the country. Discuss your feelings about these ideas. Can you think of some other ways to express support for Israel?

2. Many people were upset by Judith Kaplan Eisenstein's bat mitzvah because having a bat mitzvah was a new idea. Identify and discuss a time when your synagogue or Jewish community tried a controversial new idea.

ACTIVITIES

1. Make a wall chart that shows the ties between your community and Israel. You might want to draw a large bridge. On one end of the bridge, write the name of your community. On the other end of the bridge, draw a map of Israel. On the bridge itself, list all of the ties between the two ends. For example: People from your community who have made *aliyah*; Israelis who live in your community; Organizations that work for Israel; Exchange programs for students; Special projects like planting trees in Israel; Special fund-raising drives; Community trips to Israel; etc.

2. Use the *Encyclopaedia Judaica* to find out more about one of the following: Hadassah; the Hebrew University; Brandeis University; the Zionist Organization of America, Yeshiva University.

3. Did your mother or grandmother have a bat mitzvah? If one did, interview her, and write about how she celebrated this event. Compare her celebration with that of Judith Kaplan Eisenstein.

4. Do you believe that America should have a chief rabbi? Write two reasons why America should have a chief rabbi and two reasons why it should not. Combine your reasons with those of your classmates and then discuss all the reasons that were suggested.

SHOULD AMERICA HAVE A CHIEF RABBI?

Why?

a. _____

b. _____

Why not?

a. _____

b. _____

135

This World War II poster encouraged all Americans to join forces to win the war.

The Great Depression in the United States

Franklin D. Roosevelt is elected president

Adolf Hitler assumes power in Germany

Britain issues its White Paper on Palestine
Hitler invades Poland

World War II

United Nations votes for the establishment
of the State of Israel

Israel becomes a state

Beginning of the cold war
with the Soviet Union

Korean War

Racial segregation in public schools
is ruled unconstitutional by the
Supreme Court

1929   1932   1933   1939   1941-1945   1947   1948   1950 1953   1954

MODERN TIMES

The following chapters tell the story of American Jews before, during, and after World War II. You will learn about a government program created by President Franklin Delano Roosevelt called the New Deal and how it affected Jews. You will take pride in the heroic efforts of American Jews who sacrificed their lives in World War II. You will also learn about the many Jews whose names became household words to most Americans during these years.

After World War II, many Jews moved from the inner cities to the suburbs. You will find out how this move influenced and changed Jewish life. In 1948, Israel became a nation. You will read how American Jews contributed to that historic event.

Finally, you will learn about the 1960s to the end of the 1980s. What was Jewish life like for your parents when they were growing up? How were those times different from and similar to the years in which you are growing up? As you read, you will discover the roots of your own history.

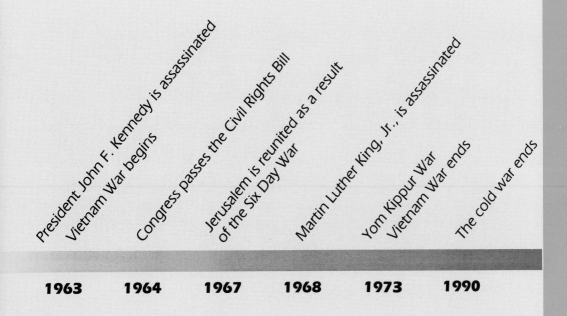

President John F. Kennedy is assassinated
Vietnam War begins
Congress passes the Civil Rights Bill
Jerusalem is reunited as a result of the Six Day War
Martin Luther King, Jr., is assassinated
Yom Kippur War
Vietnam War ends
The cold war ends

1963   **1964**   **1967**   **1968**   **1973**   **1990**

THE DEPRESSION AND WORLD WAR II

LINKS IN HISTORY

The World in Crisis

Several major world events occurred from the 1920s to 1945. In the early twenties, business was booming and people were spending large sums of money. Then came a stock market crash that resulted in a great economic depression, which lasted until the beginning of World War II.

During the 1920s, industries in the United States were producing more goods than Americans could afford to buy. As a result, people began buying items on credit. By paying a little each month, the average American worker was able to buy expensive items.

However, living on credit soon began to cause problems. People who had bought many items on credit often found that they could not pay their bills each month. When

During the Depression, thousands of people stood on breadlines.

On Kristallnacht (the "Night of Broken Glass"), November 1938, most of the synagogues in Germany were destroyed. This photograph shows the remains of one of Berlin's leading synagogues.

a business did not receive customers' payments, it, in turn, did not have the money to continue manufacturing or to buy new goods.

As a result, industries began to lay off workers in the late 1920s. Banks that had made unwise loans were not repaid. Many of them had to close. On October 29, 1929, the stock market crashed. People who had invested money in stocks found that these stocks had lost most of their value. The crash marked the beginning of the **Great Depression**. By 1932, eleven million Americans were out of work.

In 1932, Americans elected Franklin Delano Roosevelt president of the United States. Roosevelt had a plan to put the unemployed back to work. He called his plan the **New Deal**.

The depression was felt not only in America. Europe, too, suffered economically. In Germany, things were very bad. In 1933, Adolf Hitler became the leader of Germany. He led the Nazi party. Hitler promised his people that he would end the depression. He blamed the Jews for Germany's problems. Even though the Jews had lived in Germany since the time of the Romans, Hitler said that they were foreigners. Hitler planned to make Germany strong by conquering other countries. In 1939, Hitler attacked Poland. This marked the beginning of World War II, which ended in 1945.

THE JEWISH EXPERIENCE

In 1877, a wealthy Jewish banker, Joseph Seligman, arrived in Saratoga Springs, New York, in his own railroad car. He had come to vacation in this famous summer resort, as he had done for the past ten years. However, when he attempted to register as a guest at the Grand Union, the best hotel in town, he was told that "Israelites" were no longer permitted to stay there. Joseph Seligman was a victim of **anti-Semitism**, or discrimination against Jews.

ANTI-SEMITISM IN AMERICA Another well-known incident of anti-Semitism occurred in 1913. Leo Frank, a Jewish resident of Atlanta, Georgia, was accused of murdering a young Christian girl, Mary Phagan. Leo Frank was in charge of the pencil factory in which Mary Phagan worked. He was convicted and sentenced to death, based on false evidence. Some people in Atlanta who disliked Jews celebrated with a parade. Later, the governor of Georgia questioned the evidence against Frank and changed his sentence to life in prison. But a group of people broke into Frank's prison cell and hanged him. Nobody was ever brought to trial for Frank's death.

Many years later, an eyewitness to the murder of Mary Phagan came forward. At the time of Leo Frank's trial, he had been threatened with death if he told what he had seen. He finally felt that he could disclose who the murderer was. He confirmed that Leo Frank was innocent.

In the 1920s, Henry Ford, the automobile manufacturer, published *The Dearborn Independent*, a newspaper in which he wrote that the Jews were dangerous because they were plotting to dominate the world. The Jews of the United States responded by boycotting Ford cars. It was only after Henry Ford was threatened with a lawsuit by Aaron Sapiro, one of the Jews whom Ford had named, that Ford apologized and stopped publishing his newspaper.

The kind of anti-Semitism that Jews faced during these times is called **social anti-Semitism**. Jews faced discrimination

Leo Frank at his installation as president of the Atlanta B'nai B'rith in 1912.

Franklin Delano Roosevelt was elected president of the United States in 1932.

in society. They were barred from buying homes in certain areas. When Jews went to apply for some jobs, they saw signs that read "Jews and Negroes need not apply." Many colleges began using a quota system. This meant that most colleges accepted only a small number of Jewish students.

THE GREAT DEPRESSION The rise of the Nazi party in Germany and the Great Depression made matters worse for many Jews. In the United States, an organization called the German-American Bund sympathized with the Nazis. This group tried to win Americans over to the anti-Jewish ideas in which Hitler believed.

The Ku Klux Klan, an anti-black group, was also active in spreading hate literature against Jews. A Catholic priest, Father Charles Coughlin, preached anti-Semitism on the radio. Jewish organizations like the Anti-Defamation League of B'nai B'rith began to fight back. They made people aware of the groups that were spreading hatred. They also tried to educate the public about the freedoms to which all the citizens of the United States are entitled.

THE ROOSEVELT YEARS When Franklin Delano Roosevelt became the president of the United States in 1932, the Jewish community considered him their friend. Many Jews found jobs as a result of the New Deal. In addition, Roosevelt appointed Jews to help him run the government. Henry Morgenthau, Jr., became Roosevelt's secretary of the treasury.

Prejudice against Jews increased in

other parts of the world during the 1930s. In Palestine, the Arabs rioted against the Jewish settlers. In Germany, Hitler openly talked about killing the Jews. By 1939, Hitler had begun to conquer Europe. Wherever the Nazis went, they established concentration camps and imprisoned and murdered people simply because they were Jewish.

The Jews of New York City held a mass protest meeting in 1933 in Madison Square Garden. Tens of thousands of people gathered to speak out against the rise of Nazism in Germany.

WORLD WAR II America tried to stay out of World War II. However, on December 7, 1941, the Japanese, who were Germany's allies, bombed the American naval base at Pearl Harbor. America had no choice but to enter the war. Over five hundred thousand Jewish men and women enlisted in the American armed forces. They fought bravely, eager to rid the world of Nazism.

At the beginning of World War II, the situation for Jews throughout the world could not have been worse. In 1939, the British, who governed Palestine at the time, issued the **White Paper**. This was a document that greatly limited Jewish immigration to Palestine. In the United States, Congress would not change the immigration laws and refused entry to thousands of European Jews.

THE HOLOCAUST When American Jews began to hear stories about the Nazi concentration camps, they organized protest meetings. They collected money with which they hoped to buy freedom for some of the Nazis' victims. Jews asked President Roosevelt to order Allied planes to bomb the railroads that carried Jews to the death camps. But Roosevelt felt it was more important to use the planes to bomb German troops. In 1944, President Roosevelt finally established the War Refugee Board to help save Jews from the Nazis. But for millions of Jews, it was too late. When American soldiers entered the death camps, the terrible truth became public: Six million European Jews had been murdered by the Nazis. This mass murder is known as the **Holocaust**.

In 1933, tens of thousands of people marched to Madison Square Garden in New York City to demonstrate against the policies of Nazi Germany.

143

One Fateful Night

American Jews wholeheartedly supported their country during World War II. Thousands of American Jews served in the different branches of the armed forces. Many of them earned military honors for their bravery. A large number of Jewish servicemen and service-women died fighting the enemy.

Many rabbis enlisted in the armed forces as chaplains. They, too, won medals for their courage. The story you are about to read is about an especially courageous chaplain, Alexander David Goode.

Alexander was born in 1911. His parents had hoped that he would become an engi-neer, but Alexander had other plans. His grandfather and great-grandfather had been rabbis, and Alexander wanted to follow in their footsteps. He studied for the rabbinate at Hebrew Union College in Cincinnati.

After he was ordained, he became the rabbi of Temple Beth Israel in York, Penn-sylvania. Rabbi Goode worked hard to pro-mote better understanding between Chris-tians and Jews. He believed that democracy was the best form of government. To con-vince others of his beliefs, he became a Boy Scout leader. He even wrote a textbook on democracy for high schools and colleges.

"Sir, are you the Catholic chaplain?" A young sailor inched his way toward Chaplain Alexander Goode, who was holding on tightly to the rail of the troopship the *Dorchester* on a cold, windy night in the North Atlantic.

"No, I'm the Jewish chaplain," Rabbi Goode replied. "But maybe I can help you." Why aren't you below deck, asleep?"

"Chaplain, that's the problem. There is a sailor in the next bunk who doesn't let us sleep. He must be no more than eighteen years old, and he just lies there and cries. He's very scared that something awful is going to happen. The guys told me to find the Catholic chaplain, but I guess it would be all right if you came down. Maybe if you spoke to him, he would go to sleep."

"Take me to him. I'll try my best to calm him. A night this cold and windy is enough to frighten the most seasoned sailor," the chaplain replied.

Below deck, over nine hundred men were tossing and turning with each roll of the ship. They were on their way from Saint John's, Newfoundland, to Greenland. The overcast sky on this wintry cold night was pitch-black. There were rumors that enemy ships and submarines were follow-ing the *Dorchester* and the other ships in her convoy. If the rumors were true, the situation was all the more ominous be-cause even the sailors on the bridge, who were using the navy's most advanced equipment, could see nothing.

Chaplain Goode tried his best to com-fort the frightened sailor. In other bunk rooms, the Protestant chaplains Clark Pol-

ing and George Fox and the Catholic chaplain John Washington were also busy trying to calm men.

Back on deck, the four chaplains spoke of their own fears and tried to reassure one another. Suddenly, the ship was rocked by an enormous explosion.

"We've been hit broadside," cried Chaplain Poling.

Bells began to ring. "May day, may day," the captain shouted on the loudspeaker. "We've been hit by an enemy torpedo. Report to your lifeboat stations immediately. Take your life jackets with you." Then, with even greater urgency, he ordered, "Abandon ship, abandon ship."

The dazed sailors ran onto the decks. In their panic, many of them forgot their life jackets. The chaplains began to hand out jackets from the emergency boxes alongside the lifeboats. However, this supply was soon exhausted.

Again the captain's voice came over the loudspeaker. "All hands abandon ship. Everyone into the lifeboats."

"Chaplain, I'm scared," cried a young sailor. "I have no life jacket. What will happen?"

"You'll be fine. Here, take my life jacket. I'll find another one. Hurry now, into the boat with you," Chaplain Goode replied, pushing the frightened man into a lifeboat.

Each of the other chaplains had also removed his life jacket and had put it over the head of a sailor.

The ship was listing dangerously. The men were in a panic, and many of them were jumping overboard into the frigid water.

One sailor, Lieutenant John Mahoney, resisted Chaplain Goode's efforts to get him into a lifeboat.

"I left my gloves below deck," John said. "I must get them."

"No, no," Chaplain Goode replied forcefully, "there is no time to go below deck. The ship is sinking. Here, take my gloves and get into this lifeboat."

"But what will become of you?" asked the sailor. "You have no life jacket, and now you are giving me your gloves."

"I will find another life jacket, and I have another pair of gloves. You will need the gloves to help you hold on to the lifeboat. Now into the boat with you, and may God protect us all," Chaplain Goode replied.

The lifeboat pulled away from the sinking ship. As Lieutenant Mahoney looked back from the lifeboat, he saw an amazing sight. The four chaplains were standing together on the deck, their arms linked. As the boat sank, they prayed. Above the roar of the wind, John Mahoney could hear Alexander Goode's prayer. Because he did not understand Hebrew, he could not make out the words. If he had, he would have heard the chaplain chant, *"Shema Yisrael, Adonai Elohenu, Adonai Echad."* ("Hear, O Israel: *Adonai* is our God, *Adonai* is One.")

It was February 3, 1943. Of the 904 men who had been aboard the *Dorchester*, only 226 survived. Lieutenant Mahoney spent eight hours in the crowded lifeboat. After he was rescued, he said, "Without the chaplain's help, I would never have made it. As it is, only two of the forty of us who were in the lifeboat survived. I owe my life to Chaplain Goode."

Rabbi Goode was awarded the Distinguished Service Cross and the Purple Heart after his death. President Dwight D. Eisenhower proclaimed February 3, 1957, "Dorchester Day." In addition, Rabbi Goode received the Congressional Medal of Heroism.

This stamp memorializes the four chaplains who died in World War II when the *Dorchester* was hit by an enemy torpedo.

IN THEIR OWN WORDS

Orphan Children

In 1946, Rabbi Benjamin H. Gorrelick was a chaplain. He wrote about his work with Jewish orphans who had lost their parents in the Holocaust.

From June 22, 1945, to January 8, 1946, I was stationed in Brussels, Belgium. Ten Jewish orphanages were located in and around the city, housing close to two thousand boys and girls. Most of their parents had been murdered during the war.

. . . I prayed with the children and played with them. . . . The little ones hugged me and would not let me go. . . . For the High Holy Days, I held services in the large concert hall of Brussels. The more than one thousand worshipers included about two hundred older boys and girls. It was a great religious experience for the American GIs to have these young suffering brethren with them. At the end of Yom Kippur day, we invited the youngsters to break the fast with the military personnel.

. . . We had a seven-course breakfast that night—a real kosher one, with our visiting orphans as our special guests. The theme song . . . was "Next Year in Jerusalem"—the major hope of all these youngsters. Most of them did eventually settle in Palestine, where they are now part of the State of Israel.

This etching depicts the heroic educator Janusz Korczak, who ran an orphanage in the Warsaw ghetto and gave his life trying to save orphan children.

Many Famous Jews

Despite the hard times and the anti-Semitism experienced by Jews in the 1930s, many Jews succeeded in their fields and became household names.

Almost everyone has heard of Albert Einstein. Einstein was the German scientist who formulated the theory of relativity. His work paved the way for the peaceful use of atomic energy and helped America develop the atom bomb. He immigrated to the United States in the 1930s, when some Jews were still able to escape from Germany. Einstein taught at Princeton University. He was always ready to work for and support Jewish causes.

Movies were a favorite form of entertainment during these years. Many of the great Hollywood producers and actors were Jews. The famous studio of Metro-Goldwyn-Mayer is named for two Jewish producers, Louis Mayer and Samuel Goldwyn. Al Jolson, the son of a *chazan*, starred in *The Jazz Singer*, the first motion picture with sound. The movie is about a cantor's son who becomes a famous vaudeville singer.

There were also some very famous Jewish comedians at this time. The list includes Jack Benny, Fanny Brice, Milton Berle, the Marx Brothers, and Eddie Cantor.

Ernest Bloch earned fame as a composer of classical music. Aaron Copland wrote music that had beautiful American themes, like *Appalachian Spring*. One of the great jazz composers of the 1930s was George Gershwin, who wrote a well-known American opera, *Porgy and Bess*. Jerome Kern wrote Broadway musicals, including *Show Boat*. Another popular songwriter and creator of many Broadway musicals was Irving Berlin, the son of a cantor.

Bernard Baruch, who was of Sephardic descent on his mother's side and German-Polish descent on his father's side, was a friend and adviser to four presidents—Wilson, Harding, Roosevelt, and Truman. Toward the end of his life, he represented the United States as a member of the United Nations Atomic Energy Commission.

Most people know about Hank Greenberg, the star first baseman of the Detroit Tigers. There were also other Jewish sports figures. Barney Ross was a popular lightweight and welterweight champion of the 1930s. Benny Leonard was lightweight champion from 1917 to 1924. Sid Luckman played quarterback for the Chicago Bears in the 1940s.

The list of Jews who made major contributions to American life in the 1930s and 1940s goes on and on. It also includes many famous doctors, rabbis, artists, and writers. Some of their names are listed in the Activities section on page 151.

148

Albert Einstein became a United States citizen after escaping from Nazi Germany.

The Jazz Singer, starring Al Jolson, was the first motion picture with sound.

Fanny Brice, a famous comedian, was portrayed by Barbra Streisand in the musical *Funny Girl*.

Hank Greenberg, one of the greatest baseball players in major league history, played for the Detroit Tigers.

Jewish teenagers Jerome Siegel and Joe Shuster created Superman in 1939.

CHAPTER 12 ▶ CHECKUP

Reread the chapter and fill in the blanks with the correct names of famous Jews of the 1930s and 1940s.

1. A scientist who worked on theories of atomic energy._____
2. An entertainer who starred in *The Jazz Singer.*_____
3. A boxing champion._____
4. The composer of *Appalachian Spring.*_____
5. One of several comedians._____
6. The writer of a well-known American opera._____
7. A friend and adviser of presidents._____
8. A star first baseman of the Detroit Tigers._____
9. The composer of the American musical *Show Boat.*_____
10. Two men who produced movies. _____and _____
_____

DISCUSSION

1. Define the word *Holocaust.* Discuss the significance of the Holocaust in Jewish history.

2. Each year on Yom Hashoah, Holocaust Remembrance Day, services are held, programs are shown on television, and articles about the tragic events of the Nazi era are printed. Some people, both Jews and Christians, have said that there is too much remembrance. They believe that these events are long past and that people should not dwell on them. Others say the only way to insure that such evil events will not happen again is to educate and remind people of that time. Discuss this issue.

3. The Jewish slogan "Never Again" means that Jews will not stand by quietly if terrible events like those that took place during the Holocaust were to occur again. Discuss some of the ways in which you can fight anti-Semitism.

ACTIVITIES

1. Find out more about American Jews during the 1930s and 1940s. Use the names of the people that appear in this chapter, or choose from the following list.

Jacob Adler	Sophie Tucker	Ben Shahn
J. Robert Oppenheimer	Felix Frankfurter	Jacob Epstein
Alfred Stieglitz		

2. Create an American Jewish Hall of Fame. Make paper doll models of the figures and, if possible, design clothes that show each person's talent or skill. For example: Dress Hank Greenberg in the baseball uniform of the Detroit Tigers. Secure each paper doll to a small pedestal. You can make the pedestal from a half-pint milk container that you have covered with white paper. On the sides of each pedestal, outline the basic facts of the person's life and how that person contributed to American and Jewish life.

List below those people that you would nominate to the American Jewish Hall of Fame. Describe each person's contribution.

Nominee	
Contribution	

Nominee	
Contribution	

3. Create a miniature memorial to the chaplains of the *Dorchester*. Your memorial might take the form of a small stained-glass window made of bits of colored glass glued to a backing; a drawing; a clay sculpture; etc.

4. Listen to the musical arrangement of *Kol Nidre* composed by Ernest Bloch. Ask your rabbi or *chazan* to speak to the class about the origins of the *Kol Nidre* prayer.

5. Design a Holocaust program for your school for Yom Hashoah, based on the book *I Never Saw Another Butterfly*. This is a volume of poetry by children who were in a concentration camp. You might choose to recite a poem or write your own poetic answers to one or more of the poems in this book, telling the children who were in the camp about the world today.

6. Do a community survey and find out how many families in your community lost relatives during the Holocaust. If you have access to a computer, create a data base, listing the families, names, and ages of those who died, as well as their place of origin, etc. Print out this data base, and display it on Yom Hashoah.

C H A P T E R 13

YEARS OF GROWTH AND REBUILDING

LINKS IN HISTORY

The United Nations Votes for a Jewish State

When World War II ended in 1945, life in Europe was a nightmare. Millions of people had been killed. Millions more had lost their homes.

People wanted to make sure that another world war would never happen again. The United States helped form the United Nations. Its job was to keep peace in the world by providing a place for leaders to meet and discuss their differences.

One of the purposes of the United Nations was to help war victims rebuild their lives. Six million European Jews had been murdered by the Nazis. The Jews who had survived did not want to return to the countries that had failed to protect them during the war years. The nations of the world realized that Jews needed a homeland of their own.

On November 29, 1947, the United Nations voted for the establishment of a Jewish state. On May 14, 1948, Israel pro-claimed its statehood. Immediately, the Arab nations that surrounded Israel attacked. The Israelis were ready to defend themselves. They fought bravely and drove back the invaders.

In spite of the establishment of the United Nations, tensions between nations began to develop. The United States was concerned because the Soviet Union had begun to impose its Communist ideas on the countries of Eastern Europe. The United States and the Soviet Union became more and more distrustful of each other. They began to stockpile weapons. The 1950s marked the beginning of what is known as the **cold war**. Each side had its weapons ready for war at a moment's notice. War did break out in Korea in the 1950s and in Vietnam in the 1960s but was contained in those regions.

In the United States, great changes took

Hours after David Ben-Gurion read Israel's Declaration of Independence on May 14, 1948, Arab nations declared war on the Jewish state.

place after World War II. Automobiles and railroads gave people the opportunity to travel farther and to commute to their jobs. The country became prosperous. People bought homes in small towns near the big cities. These towns, called suburbs, were soon part of the metropolitan area of the cities.

THE JEWISH EXPERIENCE

In the 1950s, many American Jews began moving to the suburbs. This move paved the way for a new style of living. When Jews lived next to one another in the cities, it was easy for them to associate with other Jews and to form a community. Living in the suburbs changed Jewish communal life. Jews no longer lived near one another.

THE CHANGING JEWISH COMMUNITY
Because Jews in the suburbs began to feel the need to communicate with one another, they started to build synagogues.

Temple Oheb Shalom, in Baltimore, Maryland, was one of the hundreds of new synagogues built during the 1950s and 1960s.

Hundreds of synagogues were built during this time. The synagogues were designed to serve not only the religious needs of the members of the community but also their social and recreational needs. Perhaps your synagogue was built at this time.

Most people sent their children to the afternoon schools that these synagogues organized. Occasionally, in smaller communities, different synagogues joined together and supported community Hebrew schools. Jewish camps were very popular at this time, just as they are now.

Jews hoped that in this postwar era, they would be accepted as equals. Colleges did drop the quota system, and it became easier for Jews to find jobs. But even though Jews worked side by side with Christians, they were often discriminated against. Attempts were still made to keep Jews from buying houses in certain neighborhoods and to exclude them from certain vacation resorts.

THE COLD WAR Events occurred during the 1950s that troubled American Jews. During the cold war, many Americans were frightened and suspicious of Communists. They began to suspect other Americans of having Communist connections and sympathies.

Senator Joseph McCarthy became the head of a congressional committee to weed out American Communists. His enthusiasm soon became dangerous. He accused many people of being Communists, often on the basis of very little evidence. Teachers, writers, and actors were among the accused. As a result, many of these people lost their jobs. Some of them were Jews. Jews and other Americans became concerned that the civil rights of many people were being abused.

In one famous instance, a Jewish couple, Julius and Ethel Rosenberg, was arrested on charges that they had given the Russians atomic secrets. The Rosenbergs were tried and found guilty. The judge, Irving Kaufman, also a Jew, sentenced them to death in the electric chair. Their execution took place in 1953. This marked the first time that people accused of spying were executed in peacetime. Some people claim that the execution of the Rosenbergs was due to the anti-Communist hysteria of that time.

ISRAEL On May 14, 1948, David Ben-Gurion proudly proclaimed the establishment of the State of Israel. All over America, Jews listened to their radios as Ben-Gurion read the historic proclamation. Many American Jewish leaders contributed to this great event. Abba Hillel Silver, a Reform rabbi, was the American spokesman for the Jewish Agency, the group that handled

Israelis celebrate their country's Independence Day by dancing in the streets.

matters relating to Palestine. As a representative of the Jewish people, he frequently addressed the United Nations, where he spoke out for the creation of a Jewish state.

Upon hearing Ben-Gurion's proclamation, Jews in cities and towns across the United States poured out of their homes and began to dance in the streets. People laughed and cried with joy as they hugged one another and spoke about the miracle that they were privileged to witness. Not since the year 135 C.E. had there been a Jewish government in the land of Israel.

Cindy's Choice

Growing up Jewish in small cities and towns throughout the United States in the 1950s was not much different from the way it is today. Jewish children met one another in religious schools, synagogues, and youth groups. Many Jewish children attended summer camps, just as they do today.

However, some major differences existed in the way Christians and Jews lived together at that time. Jews had just begun to stand up for their beliefs when they found themselves in conflict with some of the customs of the larger population. Often it was the children who had to decide how to express their Judaism. They felt uncomfortable when Christmas hymns were sung in their classrooms or when prayers were said at the beginning of the school day. Many times, teachers scheduled tests on Jewish holidays.

In the following story, you will read about some of the problems that Jewish children faced during that time. As you read the story, think about how some things are the same today and how some things have changed.

Until this week, thirteen-year old Cindy could not remember a time in her life when she had been unhappy. Now suddenly, several things had happened all at once. Cindy was no longer so sure that life was a breeze, as she had once told her best friend, Gail.

Gail often moped about things, and Cindy always felt that it was her duty to cheer her friend up. Now it was Cindy who needed cheering up.

It was a warm Friday evening, unusual for the middle of a September in New England. The leaves on the elm trees in front of the house had just begun to turn colors. Cindy sat on her porch swing, thinking about the events of the past week.

School had begun the week before. That was the core of the problem. If only camp could have gone on and on. Cindy loved the Jewish summer camp that she went to. She found it much easier to accept the rules of the camp one hundred miles away in southern New Hampshire than to accept her parents' rules.

The best day in camp was Shabbat. There was singing and outdoor services. Everyone dressed alike in the blue-and-white camp uniform. The counselors who led the services were not only cute but seemed to be so self-confident. Cindy wondered if confidence comes when you are seventeen. At thirteen, she could not imagine that she would ever be like them.

When school started, Hebrew school also began. Cindy enjoyed Hebrew school. She had become a bat mitzvah the year before, and she now attended a confirmation class. She liked Hebrew school for the same reason that she enjoyed camp. The teacher told wonderful stories, and Cindy found that she could express herself in a small class in a way that she was not able to in her large classes at the junior high school.

School had started right after Labor

Day. Cindy looked forward to her classes, especially to her mathematics class. She was a math whiz, and she was excited about taking algebra for the first time.

At the end of the first week, however, Cindy was shocked when on Thursday, Miss Noble announced, "Class, we will have our first math quiz next Monday. Make sure that you do your homework in preparation."

"Monday," Cindy thought. "Monday is Rosh Hashanah."

"Miss Noble," Cindy said, as the class was leaving the room, "Monday is a Jewish holiday. I am afraid that I cannot take the quiz. Can I make it up?"

"Absolutely not," Miss Noble replied unkindly. "In my class, I expect everyone to take the tests as scheduled, unless he or she has a doctor's notice."

"But I won't be sick, Miss Noble," Cindy said softly. "I cannot come to school because Monday is Rosh Hashanah, the Jewish New Year."

"I don't care what it is," replied Miss Noble. "If you are absent for the quiz without a doctor's notice, you will get a zero." Having said this, Miss Noble brushed past Cindy and left the room.

Cindy met Gail at the lockers and told her what Miss Noble had said. "You are so lucky that you have Mr. Wayne for math, Gail. At least he isn't giving a quiz on Rosh Hashanah."

"Cheer up, Cindy," Gail said, trying to be helpful. "Guess what? I just met Chuck Richards. He said that the people on his block are organizing a huge tag sale on Saturday. They need all the kids they can get to help sell stuff. He invited us to come and work."

"I don't think that my mom will let me go," Cindy replied.

"Why in the world not?" asked Gail. "We've been hoping that Chuck's group would ask us to join them. You were the one who wondered if we were being excluded because we are Jewish. Now's our chance. Why won't your mom let you work?"

"Because Saturday is Shabbat, and my mom expects me to go to synagogue," Cindy replied.

"Your mom is so old-fashioned. My family has gotten away from all that religious stuff ages ago. Why don't you tell her everyone will be there? Besides, we are getting paid for helping out."

"That's just it. It is not right to work on Shabbat," Cindy said. "I wish I were back in camp. Shabbat was so nice there, and there were no problems."

"Think about it, Cindy," Gail said, as she went off to her next class. "It's our big chance. I'm going, no matter what."

"Hey, Cindy," Joan Richards greeted her in history class. "I hear that my brother invited you to help us on Saturday. I hope you'll come." Joan's last words sounded more like a dare than an invitation.

"I'm not sure, Joan. I'll see what my mom says," Cindy replied.

"I told my brother that he shouldn't expect much if he invites you to help out," Joan said in a low voice, almost as if she were talking to herself. But Cindy knew that Joan had intended her words to be heard. Cindy felt her face getting red. Before she could ask Joan to explain her remark, however, history class began.

After school, Cindy told her mom about Miss Noble's test on Rosh Hashanah.

"Dad and I will go see the principal tomorrow," Mom said. "It is time that we complained about the fact that teachers schedule tests on Jewish holidays. I will call the rabbi. Perhaps if a group of Jewish parents join together, the schools will be more sensitive to the needs of Jewish kids."

"But Mom, I don't want to start a big thing. I know that it is not right for Jewish kids to get zeros because they observe the holidays. But I also don't want the other kids to say that I'm different."

"Cindy, you know that I did not grow up in this country. Your father and I came from Poland before the war. When we became Americans, we thought people would forget that we are Jewish. The war and the terrible things that happened in Europe have taught us that no one forgets that you are Jewish. In America, the difference is that we can fight for our rights. When people see that we are ready to stand up for ourselves, perhaps they will have more respect for our traditions."

"I don't know, Mom," Cindy replied. "Something else also happened in school, today." Cindy told her mom about Chuck's invitation to work at the tag sale on Saturday.

"Cindy, you know your father and I do not work on Shabbat, but you will have to decide what you want to do. You are old enough to make your own decisions. I have often heard from you how much Shabbat meant to you in camp. But you must realize that Shabbat is more than just singing beautiful songs. It is a way of living. You will have to decide. If you want these people to be your friends, perhaps you can go but not work. From Joan's remark, however, I am not sure what kind of friends they would be. Think about it."

Mom, Dad, and the rabbi went to the principal the next morning. The principal listened to their request and promised to speak to the teachers about not scheduling tests on religious holidays. He asked the rabbi for a Jewish calendar so he could make sure the situation would not arise again. In the meantime, he told Cindy not to worry. He would see to it that her grades would not suffer if she could not make up the test.

Cindy decided on her own that she would not work on Shabbat. She wanted very much to keep the special Shabbat feeling that she had experienced in camp. If going to services was the only way she could keep that feeling, that was where she wanted to be. But the events of the week still depressed her. As she sat on the porch, they kept going through her mind.

"Cindy?" Joan was walking up the porch stairs. "Chuck tells me that you can't work tomorrow. You know, at first I was annoyed because I felt that you were snubbing us. But then Gail explained to me why you won't come. I came over to apologize. I didn't know that you are religious. My grandmother is very religious, too, and she is always asking my mother why I don't attend church every Sunday. I know I should go more often. I'll tell you what. Perhaps one Saturday morning, you will invite me to your synagogue. I've never been to a Jewish service and I'm curious."

"I would really like that," Cindy said.

Mickey Marcus

Mickey Marcus.

On May 14, 1948, the day on which Israel declared statehood, the armies of seven Arab countries attacked. The Israelis, who knew that the Arabs would invade, had been preparing for this moment. Many young Jews had received their military training in an underground army called the Haganah. During the years of the British occupation of Palestine, the **Haganah** and other underground military groups had helped bring European refugees to Palestine. They had also helped the Jewish farmers defend themselves against Arab raiders. Now their members joined to form the army of Israel.

The Israelis knew that if their small army was going to stand up against the Arab fighters who outnumbered them, it had to be commanded by the best military experts they could find.

The year before Israel became a state, the search for a top military adviser had begun. Israeli officials came to the United States and asked Colonel David Daniel Marcus, a graduate of the United States Military Academy at West Point, to help them. Colonel Marcus, whose nickname was Mickey, accepted the assignment. He had always hoped that the Jewish people would return to their homeland, and he loved a challenge.

Mickey Marcus was born in New York City in 1902. He was a bright student and an excellent athlete. Mickey entered West Point in 1920, where he is remembered as a gymnast and a welterweight boxing champion. After three years in the army, he decided to become a lawyer.

When World War II began, Mickey Marcus reenlisted in the army. He took part in the D-day invasion of France and fought bravely. He was one of the first American soldiers to enter Dachau, the German concentration camp. What he saw there horrified him.

In Israel, he earned a reputation as a daring military planner. He soon became commander of the brigade that was fighting to free Jerusalem from the Jordanians. He was the first officer to be awarded the rank of brigadier general. Mickey ordered that a special road be built so that the Israelis could secretly transport men and supplies to the outskirts of the city.

In June 1948, Mickey and his men were camped in a village called Abu Ghosh, which is now part of Jerusalem. One night, he had difficulty falling asleep. As he tossed and turned, he thought about the hard times that still lay ahead. "Enough of this," he said to himself. "Some fresh air will make me sleepy." He arose and went out into the moonless night. An Israeli sentry on guard duty called out, "Who goes there?" Perhaps the Hebrew-speaking sentry did not understand or hear the commander's answer because he raised his rifle and shot into the air. When the figure in the darkness did not stop moving toward him, the sentry fired again. This time, the bullet fatally struck Mickey Marcus.

All of Israel mourned Mickey's death. His body was taken back to the United States and buried with military honors in the cemetery at West Point. Many American and Israeli officials came to pay their respects to Mickey Marcus. They remembered Colonel Marcus as a man who had enormous energy and courage. An American movie was made about his life. In Israel, a village, Mishmar David, is named for this brave Jewish soldier.

IN THEIR OWN WORDS

Being Jewish at West Point

Dr. Emanuel Neumann, a Zionist leader, tells the following story about Colonel Mickey Marcus.

West Point required the students to attend chapel services. . . . When Mickey came home on his first furlough, he was interrogated by his grandmother. He had to give her a "blow-by-blow" account of his life and doings at West Point. . . . When he told her about his attendance at Christian services in the chapel, she was horrified. "You are a Jewish boy," she exclaimed, "and you have no business going to chapel! You must cut it out or come back home."

When he returned to school and failed to attend chapel, he was summoned to the office of the superintendent and asked to explain his absence. He told his story truthfully. The officer listened to him gravely and came up with an answer. "Very well," he said, "you will be excused from chapel. Instead, we will arrange for you to get daily instruction from the Jewish chaplain in your own religion."

And so it was that for several years, Mickey was taught by a Jewish chaplain and received a good Jewish education—including the study of talmudic law. The superintendent responsible for Mickey's Jewish education was Colonel Douglas MacArthur, who became a famous five-star general and led the American forces in the Pacific during World War II.

Fill in the blanks to complete a summary of events in Jewish history in the late 1940s and 1950s.

World War II ended in _____. Millions of European Jews had been killed in _____ camps. In America, Jews began to leave the cities and move to the _____. They built _____. These buildings met the religious as well as the _____ and _____ needs of the members of the community.

In 1948, _____ was declared a state. An American Jewish colonel, _____, went to Israel to help the new country build an army. He died in an accident and is buried at _____.

The 1950s were known as the period of the _____ war. Many people were afraid that Communists would take over America. A famous spy case involved a Jewish couple, _____ and _____.

DISCUSSION

1. Some people live in large cities and have many Jewish neighbors. Others live in small communities, where very few people are Jewish. Do you think that it is more difficult to live a Jewish life in a small community or in a city?

2. Abba Hillel Silver and David Ben-Gurion had a disagreement. After the establishment of the State of Israel, David Ben-Gurion argued that Jews living outside Israel should be known as "friends of Israel" but should have no say in the country's politics. Abba Hillel Silver thought that Jews who worked for Israel but lived outside her borders should be allowed to help make that country's policy. Many American Jews today have various opinions about Israel's relations with her Arab neighbors. Do you think that Jews who do not live in Israel should voice their opinions about Israeli affairs? Do you think that Israelis should pay special attention to these ideas?

ACTIVITIES

1. Many of you have been to summer camp. Form groups and use the chart below to design an ideal Jewish camp. Besides the usual sports and recreational activities, be sure to include Jewish study sessions. Explain how Shabbat will be observed, and include a plan for the services. Don't forget to make a sample menu. Design a camp brochure in which you outline these programs. Give the camp a Jewish name. After your group is finished, display your brochure, along with those of the other groups. Invite another class to view the display, and let them vote for the camp that has the most to offer.

CAMP _____

Sports

_____

_____

Jewish Studies

_____

_____

_____

How Shabbat is observed _____

_____

Other programs _____

_____

2. Become a pen pal with an Israeli student. Your teacher can help you find an Israeli pen pal.

3. Have you ever had to make a choice between going along with the crowd or sticking to your Jewish beliefs? Write a story about a time when you had to make a personal decision regarding the practice of Judaism.

163

CIVIL RIGHTS FOR ALL

LINKS IN HISTORY

Decades of Change

Many important events have taken place from the 1960s to the present. In the 1960s, the civil rights movement and the Vietnam War had a major impact on the history of the United States.

In 1954, a famous case came before the Supreme Court. It is known as *Brown* versus *Board of Education.* Linda Brown, a fourth-grade African-American, wanted to go to school within walking distance of her home. The problem was that this school was for whites only. Her parents went to court to force the school to accept their daughter. The Browns took the case all the way to the Supreme Court, which ruled that segregated schools were not legal.

In 1954, the Supreme Court ruled that segregated schools, like the one pictured here, were illegal.

Reverend Martin Luther King, Jr., Reverend Ralph Abernathy, Rabbi Maurice N. Eisendrath, and Rabbi Abraham J. Heschel protested against the Vietnam War in a silent prayer vigil at Arlington National Cemetery, Washington, 1968.

Until this time, blacks had to endure many forms of segregation and bias. Besides having to attend separate schools, they had to sit in the back of buses. Water fountains and public bathrooms displayed labels that read Negros Only and Whites Only. Although this form of segregation was more common in the South, blacks in the North had difficulty finding housing in white neighborhoods. When they applied for higher-paying work, they often were turned away because of their color.

Linda Brown's case paved the way for the civil rights movement in the 1960s. Blacks began to stand up for their rights as citizens of the United States. Martin Luther King, Jr., a black civil rights leader, believed that his people could achieve equal rights by nonviolent means. His message inspired blacks and whites throughout the United States to work for an end to discrimination in housing, schools, and jobs.

The 1960s are remembered as a time of change and of great hope. When John F. Kennedy, a young, dynamic Massachusetts senator was elected president, people were filled with hope for the future. But hope soon turned to sadness. President Kennedy, his brother Senator Robert Kennedy, and Martin Luther King, Jr., were all assassinated. The 1960s were also a time of great anger. America became involved in an unpopular war in Vietnam. Groups of people, especially college students, protested against the war by holding sit-ins and rallies.

In the 1970s and 1980s, America began to change as new immigrants from Asia, Africa, and South America arrived. They brought with them religions like Buddhism and Islam. America was no longer a Christian country but a land of many religions and cultures. A society in which many groups live and work together is called a pluralistic society. During these decades, America struggled to become a more open, pluralistic society.

165

Reverend Martin Luther King, Jr., Rabbi Joachim Prinz, and others met with President John F. Kennedy in 1963, when they marched in Washington for civil rights.

THE JEWISH EXPERIENCE

By the 1960s, American Jews felt that they had achieved equal rights. Colleges no longer had quota systems that kept Jewish students from entering the college of their choice. Jews did not feel that they were being discriminated against in business.

THE CIVIL RIGHTS MOVEMENT While Jews were pleased that they had achieved equal rights, they believed that no one could feel secure if any one group in a society was not free.

Many Jews played an active part in the civil rights movement. Rabbi Maurice Eisendrath, president of the Union of American Hebrew Congregations, spoke out against bigotry and racial hatred. In 1963, a large number of Jews participated in a famous civil rights march in Washington, D.C. On that day, Rabbi Joachim Prinz, president of the American Jewish Congress, reminded his audience that to remain silent when other people are being wronged is the greatest wrong of all.

In 1965, when southern states were making it difficult for blacks to register to vote, Jews marched with blacks from Selma to Montgomery, Alabama, to protest this injustice. Rabbi Abraham Joshua Heschel, a revered teacher at the Jewish Theological Seminary, led the march, arm in arm with Martin Luther King, Jr., and other leaders.

Jews did more than march. Two young

Jews, Michael Schwerner and Andrew Goodman, along with a third civil rights worker, James Earl Chaney, a black, were among those who went to Mississippi to help blacks register to vote. Threats had been made against northerners who worked with black southern communities. The three civil rights workers were kidnapped and murdered by racists who wanted to put an end to their activities.

THE SIX DAY WAR

The establishment of the State of Israel has given all Jews a greater sense of security. Throughout history, Jews were either pitied or persecuted because they did not have a homeland. The establishment of the Jewish state in 1948 changed this. In 1967, several of the countries that surrounded Israel threatened to destroy that nation. Israel successfully defended herself against her Arab neighbors in a war that lasted just six days. Israel's victory in the Six Day War enabled the Jewish state to secure and expand her borders and to liberate the old city of Jerusalem.

THE YOM KIPPUR WAR

On Yom Kippur in 1973, Egypt and Syria attacked Israel without warning. Again, Israel successfully defended her borders. American Jews were on their way to synagogues when they heard the news of the invasion. They responded to the crisis by contributing millions of dollars to the United Jewish Appeal to help Israel defend herself. Many American Jews went to Israel to work as volunteers. They filled positions left empty when Israelis went off to fight. Some Americans enlisted as soldiers in the Israeli army. After the war, American Jews built bridges of friendship to Israel. Thousands

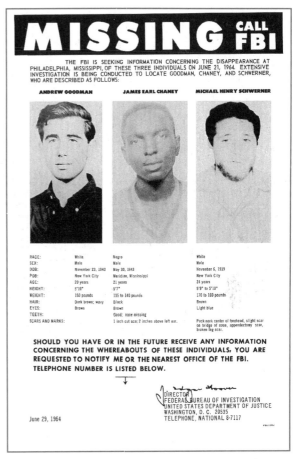

Civil rights activists Andrew Goodman, James Earl Chaney, and Michael Schwerner were murdered by white racists in 1964.

Israeli soldiers reached the Wailing Wall during the Six Day War in 1967.

American Jews held many protests on behalf of oppressed Jews in the Soviet Union.

of them visited the country as tourists and students.

During the 1970s and 1980s, Jewish lobbyists in Washington worked hard to gain support for Israel in the Senate and House of Representatives. The United States government gave Israel millions of dollars in aid to help her secure her borders and establish herself economically.

SOVIET JEWS During the 1960s, Jews in America began to turn their attention to their fellow Jews in the USSR (Union of Soviet Socialist Republics, the name of the former union of Russia and fourteen republics). The USSR at that time was a closed society. People were not free to express themselves. The government did not permit its citizens to travel or immigrate to other countries. It discouraged its people from practicing religion. The Jews in Russia were discriminated against because of their religion. Large numbers of them wished to immigrate to Israel and to America but were forbidden to do so.

American Jews held many rallies and demonstrations on behalf of Soviet Jewry. The pressure that American Jews put on the Russians began to pay off. Gradually, the USSR started to relax its strict immigration policies. Many Russian Jews were at last allowed to immigrate to Israel and to America. However, full freedom of religion and immigration was not achieved during the 1960s.

JUST YESTERDAY In the 1970s and 1980s, Jews in the United States lived well. More Jews went to college than had ever gone before. In addition, many business and professional opportunities were open to Jews.

During those years, Jews did not forget the six million Jews who had been murdered in the Holocaust. American Jews established Holocaust memorials and held teach-ins in the belief that people who remember the past will never allow such terrible events to happen again.

This Time It Was Different

Can lightning strike twice in the same place? That was the question that the Jews of Atlanta asked themselves one October morning in 1958. They had awoken to the dreadful news that their temple had been bombed.

As they dressed and rushed out to see the damage that the bomb had done, they thought of the Leo Frank case of 1913. Leo Frank was the Jewish man who had been falsely accused of murdering a young factory girl. Just as he had begun his prison term, a mob lynched him. That incident had shaken the Jewish community.

During the 1950s and 1960s, Jacob Rothschild, the rabbi of The Temple in Atlanta, refused to remain silent on the issues of segregation and equal rights. At times, his speaking out for what he believed to be just and right caused members of his congregation to ask him to be cautious. They feared that the rabbi's controversial opinions would result in anti-Semitic attacks.

Their fears came true. But the final chapter to this story is very different from that of the Leo Frank case. Read to find out what happened.

Early Sunday morning on October 12, 1958, the telephone woke Rabbi Rothschild from a deep sleep. He picked up the phone quickly, hoping that the call had not disturbed Janice, his wife.

"Oh, no," he exclaimed. "I'll be right down."

"Jack, who was that calling at this hour?" Janice asked.

"It was Robert Benton, the custodian of The Temple. Janice, The Temple has been bombed."

"Bombed? Is anyone hurt? Is there much damage?" Janice asked in a horrified voice.

"Thank God, no one was injured," Rabbi Rothschild said, as he dressed hastily. "But the rear wall, the stained-glass sanctuary window, the children's choir robes and their books are all gone. Tell whoever calls that I'm on my way," the rabbi said, as he rushed out the door.

"Mommy, what's happening?" ten-year-old Marcia stumbled into the room. Behind her was her brother, Bill, who was nine years old.

"Why did Dad run out of the house so early, Mom?" Bill asked. "What's going on?"

"Children," Janice answered, putting her arms around the two of them, "someone bombed The Temple during the night. Mr. Benton says the bomb damaged the rear of the building."

"The religious school meets in the rooms in the back of the building. What if someone had thrown that bomb while we were in school?" Bill was frightened.

"Can we go see?" Marcia asked in a teary voice.

"No, not now," Janice replied. "There will be police and fire officials there. It's better not to get in their way. But why don't you get on your bikes and spread the word about what has happened? Go to the houses of people who have children in the religious school. Tell them not to come to school today."

When Rabbi Rothschild arrived at The Temple, he was immediately surrounded by many of his congregants. Their faces showed deep fear.

Crowds of people began to gather. The police chief, reporters, photographers, and television cameramen were all there. Soon the mayor of Atlanta joined them.

"Mayor Hartsfield, do you have a message for the press?" a reporter asked.

"This bombing is the result of rabble-rousing. Rabbi Rothschild has worked hard to improve relations between blacks and whites in this city," the mayor said. "Write that it is high time that the decent people of the South follow the example that Rabbi Rothschild has set. The city of Atlanta is offering a reward for information leading to the arrest of those who planted this bomb."

The president and the vice president of The Temple also had a message for the press. They said, "We are shocked and sick at heart at the damage to our house of worship. We thank God that the explosion happened before our children and teachers arrived for Sunday school this morning."

Back at the Rothschild house, Janice and her friend Julie were busy answering phone calls. Even President Dwight D. Eisenhower telephoned to say how shocked he was. He promised that the FBI would help the local police investigate the case.

By late afternoon, when Janice felt that

Rabbi Jacob Rothschild (*above, right*) and Atlanta Mayor William Hartsfield examine the rubble after The Temple was bombed on October 12, 1958.

she could not bear to take another call, the phone rang again. She picked up the receiver.

A man's voice said, "I'm one of them that bombed your church. I'm calling to tell you there's a bomb under your house and it's lit. You've got five minutes to get out and save your life."

It took Janice a second to react. Julie saw her face go white. "Janice, who was that?" she asked.

"A man who says that there is a bomb under the house," Janice stammered. "He says it's about to explode. We've got to get out." The two women grabbed the children and ran from the house.

They went to a neighbor's house and telephoned the police. It took several minutes before they realized that the phone call had been just a threat. The house was not going to blow up. But Janice was able to describe the man's voice to the police.

The long day ended. The police posted guards at the Rothschild house. Still, the children were very frightened.

Janice said to her children, "I want you to go to Grandma's tonight. The phone will keep you up if you stay here."

"Please, Mommy, don't make us go," Marcia begged. "I'm afraid someone will try to hurt you. I won't be able to sleep at Grandma's."

"It's all right now," their father replied, hugging them. "No one is going to hurt us. There are guards here. If it will make you feel better, you can sleep here tonight."

Many weeks later, several suspects were arrested in connection with the bombing.

At their trial, Janice identified one of the suspects as the man who had called her with the bomb threat.

The jury, however, was not convinced that these suspects were the bombers. They returned a verdict of not guilty.

The Jews of Atlanta were very upset. They remembered the stories that their parents had told them about the Leo Frank case. They were afraid that the people of Atlanta would be happy that the jury had found the suspects not guilty. But this time, the people of Atlanta reacted differently.

Hundreds of them wrote to Rabbi Rothschild, telling him how sorry they were that such a horrible thing had occurred. Many people sent money to help The Temple rebuild its sanctuary.

Rabbi Rothschild told his congregation, "The blame is not only on those who did the bombing. It rests equally with those good and decent people who choose to remain silent in such a time. Too many of us, motivated by fear, led by the desire to be comfortable and safe, have failed to live by the ideals that we know to be right and good."

A Christian minister told Rabbi Rothschild, "It is a sin to destroy a house of God. It makes no difference that the members of this house are Jewish."

This incident made the Jews of Atlanta realize that times had changed and that people there did not feel the same way their ancestors had felt in 1913 when they had shouted for joy at Leo Frank's conviction. Americans were becoming more tolerant of one another.

Abraham Joshua Heschel

Professor Abraham Joshua Heschel.

Abraham Joshua Heschel was a great teacher, a rabbinical scholar, and a major religious philosopher. As a teacher, Heschel influenced hundreds of students in their study of Torah. As a scholar and philosopher, he wrote many thoughtful books about God, the prophets of the Bible, and Shabbat.

Heschel was born in Warsaw, Poland, in 1907. His ancestors included many famous rabbis. In 1940, he immigrated to the United States to escape the Nazis. For five years, he was a professor of philosophy at Hebrew Union College in Cincinnati, Ohio. From 1945 until his death in 1972, he taught at the Jewish Theological Seminary in New York City.

Abraham Joshua Heschel not only taught with words. He also taught through actions. He felt strongly that all people are important to God. To demonstrate how he felt, he played a leading role in the civil rights movement. He also held discussions with Catholic leaders in the Vatican. Together, they tried to find ways to promote better understanding and respect between Jews and Catholics.

IN THEIR OWN WORDS

Thoughts of Abraham Joshua Heschel

Rabbi Abraham Joshua Heschel wrote many books and essays. Here is how he phrased some of his beliefs about human rights.

The way we act, the way we fail to act, is a disgrace that must not go on forever. This is not a white man's world. This is not a colored man's world. It is God's world. No man has a place in this world who tries to keep another man in his place. It is time for the white man to repent.

What is the meaning of integration? To integrate means to unite, to form into a whole. Integration means fellowship, mutual respect, and concern. . . . It will be attained by sharing moments of joy, cultural values, insights, commitments.

173

Ruth Bader Ginsburg

Ruth Bader Ginsburg.

On October 1, 1993, Ruth Bader Ginsburg became the first Jewish woman associate justice of the United States Supreme Court. Justice Ginsburg joins another woman on the court, Justice Sandra Day O'Connor. They are two of the nine members of our nation's highest court.

All her life, Justice Ginsburg has fought for equal rights. After graduating at the top of her class from Columbia University Law School in 1959, she could not find a job practicing law because she was a woman. Instead, she took jobs teaching law at various universities. She pledged to work for equality for women in all professions and devoted herself to this cause.

When President Bill Clinton nominated Judge Ginsburg, he praised her as a feminist pioneer who "has repeatedly stood for the individual, the person less well-off, the outsider in society. I have no doubt," he added, "that Ruth Bader Ginsburg will be a great justice."

Madeleine May Kunin

Madeleine May Kunin.

Many Jews hold government positions. There are Jewish senators and congressmen in Washington. There are Jewish governors of states. There are Jewish mayors of American cities. These people are very concerned with solving the problems of American life. Many of them are committed Jews. They belong to synagogues, work on behalf of Israel, and cherish the values of Judaism.

Madeleine May Kunin, a past governor of Vermont, is one of these Jews. She was the first Jewish woman governor. Madeleine Kunin was also the first woman in United States history to serve three terms as governor, from 1985 to 1991. In 1993, she was appointed deputy secretary of education by President Bill Clinton.

Governor Kunin has a strong Jewish identity. She and her husband have four children who attended religious school. She often speaks to Jewish organizations around the country, many of which have given her awards. She also holds honorary degrees from several schools of higher Jewish learning, such as Yeshiva University in New York.

A. Match each name on the left with the items on the right.

1. Jacob Rothschild ———————Supreme Court case

2. Martin Luther King, Jr. ———————Supreme Court justice

3. Abraham Joshua Heschel ———————Religious philosopher

4. Linda Brown ———————Governor of Vermont

5. Madeleine Kunin ———————Nonviolent protest

6. Ruth Bader Ginsburg ———————The Temple, Atlanta, Georgia

B. As you have read, the 1960s were filled with emotion. On the chart, list each of the happenings below under the heading where you think it belongs. You might want to list some of the happenings under more than one heading. When you finish, discuss why you put the happenings where you did.

1. Desegregation of schools
2. Bombing of The Temple
3. Antiwar rallies
4. Rallies for Russian Jews
5. Discrimination in housing
6. Equal rights
7. Murder of civil rights workers
8. Assassination of President Kennedy
9. Building bridges of friendship to Israel
10. Interfaith dialogue

HOPE	SADNESS	ANGER	CHANGE

DISCUSSION

1. How do people of different races and religions get to know one another in your community? Does your synagogue participate in interfaith programs?

2. Is there a section of your community that is almost all Jewish? Are there sections that are mainly inhabited by other groups? Discuss the pros and cons of living with people who are just like you.

3. Jews played a very active role in the civil rights movement of the 1960s. Do you think that it is important for Jews to work for the civil rights of other minority groups, or should Jews work only for their own civil rights?

ACTIVITIES

1. Create a Getting to Know You box. In the box, put items that tell about you as a Jewish person. Write a card for each item that explains its purpose.

2. Create an American Jewish Heroes Day Fair. Beginning with Chapter 11, make a list of the famous American Jews that appear in this book. To do this activity, scan the pages and write down the names of the people and the reasons for their fame. With a partner, choose one of the people listed and research his or her life.

After you have gathered all of your information, think of an interesting way to display your work. You can create a picture collage; outline information on large oaktag, using colored markers; or write a newspaper story. Invite parents and friends to your American Jewish Heroes Day Fair.

C O N C L U S I O N

The Jewish Future in America

You have come to the end of this history of Jews in America. In this final chapter, you will learn about Jewish life today. You will also look into the future and imagine what the American Jewish experience will be like in the twenty-first century.

Today, American Jews form the largest Jewish community in the world. Judaism has become a mainstream religion in America. It is one of the major religions practiced in the United States and is an important part of American culture.

JEWISH POPULATION GROWTH Since the first twenty-three Jews arrived in New Amsterdam in 1654, the Jewish population in America has grown to about six million people. Will the Jewish community continue to grow, or will our population get smaller? According to some experts, the number of Jews in the United States will get smaller in the future. Two of the reasons may be that Jewish families are having fewer children and many Jews are marrying people of other religions. If these trends continue at today's fast rate, the

Rabbi Alexander M. Schindler, president of UAHC, leads a school seder.

important role that the Jewish community has played in American life may also decline. Helping the Jewish population grow is one of the challenges of the twenty-first century.

DIFFERENT FACES OF JUDAISM Synagogues in the United States are either Reform, Conservative, Orthodox, or Reconstructionist. The original handful of synagogues that existed in the American colonies has increased to over two thousand five hundred synagogues throughout the United States.

Although each religious group is devoted to its own expression of Judaism, the groups have learned from one another. For example, the bat mitzvah ceremony, which was developed by Mordecai Kaplan, has been adopted by each movement. Reform Jews were the first to ordain women as rabbis and cantors. Now the Conservative

Sally Priesand made history when she became the first woman ordained as a rabbi.

movement also follows this practice. Both the Reform and the Conservative movements have set up day schools of their own, based on the successful Orthodox *yeshivot*.

The synagogue movements will face many challenges in the years to come. As in the past, synagogues will have to adapt to the changing needs of American Jews. Today, less than half of American Jews are synagogue members. Jewish leaders are aware that Jews who do not identify with a synagogue are less likely to contribute to the Jewish community. In order to insure that Jewish life in America stays strong in the twenty-first century, synagogues will need to find ways to attract new members.

JEWS AROUND THE WORLD You have read about the mass immigration of Jews to the United States from countries in which they had been persecuted. In the last few decades, many American Jews have worked hard to help their fellow Jews emigrate from countries that were oppressing them. In recent years, hundreds of thousands of Jews from the former Soviet Union have immigrated to the United States and Israel.

In Ethiopia, Jews were caught in a civil war and a famine and received no help from an uncaring government. American and Israeli Jews have worked to bring thousands of these Ethiopian Jews to Israel. In one dramatic weekend in June 1991, fourteen thousand Ethiopian Jews were airlifted to Israel.

In several countries around the world, like Syria and Iran, Jews still live in fear of anti-Semitism and are not free to emigrate. In the years to come, Jews around the world will continue to look to American Jews for support.

Many Jews have made major contributions to these fields.

Leonard Bernstein was a world-famous conductor and the composer of many classical works, as well as the musical *West Side Story*.

Barbra Streisand directed the films *Yentel* and *Prince of Tides*. She is also a singer and has starred in many movies.

Isaac Bashevis Singer won the Nobel Prize in literature in 1978.

During her career, Beverly Sills was one of America's greatest opera singers.

Paul Simon is an award-winning singer and songwriter.

Judy Blume is the author of many books for children and young adults.

Filmmaker Steven Spielberg directed *E.T.*, *Raiders of the Lost Ark*, *Jurassic Park*, and *Schindler's List*.

AMERICAN ZIONISM The birth of the State of Israel is one of the most important events in Jewish history. American Jews have played an important part in supporting Israel. Today, thousands of American Jews work for and donate money to organizations such as Hadassah, the Zionist Organization of America (ZOA), the Association of Reform Zionists of America (ARZA), and the American Israel Public Affairs Committee (AIPAC.) Many American Jews also give money to the United Jewish Appeal (UJA) to help support programs in Israel.

Today, as in the past, Israel seeks peace with her Arab neighbors. American Jews will continue to play a key role in helping promote the peace process and assuring Israel's security.

EDUCATION Jewish education in the United States has come a long way since the first Sunday school organized by Rebecca Gratz. Today, there are more schools and Jewish education programs in America than anywhere else in the world outside Israel. These include hundreds of day schools sponsored by the major Jewish religious groups; thousands of afternoon schools and Sunday schools; and schools of higher learning, like Yeshiva University and Brandeis University. Many universities and colleges have departments of Jewish studies, where students can learn about Judaism from scholars. In addition, there are Jewish seminaries where people can

study to become a rabbi, a cantor, or an educator. In the future, the growth of Jewish study in America will depend on the continued support of its Jews.

SOCIAL ACTION As you have seen, many Jews have taken a leading role in shaping democracy in America. Today, Jews are very active in politics and government. Many Jews, such as Joseph Lieberman, the United States senator from Connecticut, and Barbara Boxer and Diane Feinstein, the United States senators from California, are members of the United States Congress. Others, like Richard Reich, secretary of labor, and Madeleine Kunin, deputy secretary of education, hold high positions in President Clinton's administration. Jewish organizations, such as the Religious Action Center of Reform Judaism and the Anti-Defamation League of B'nai B'rith, lobby in Washington for civil and religious rights. In the future, America will continue to face many issues, including racial justice, civil liberties, the environment, and the economy. As in the past, American Jews will speak out on these issues and contribute to American democracy.

THE FUTURE History is the story of people's lives—their ideals and their actions. Throughout this book, you have seen how people have changed the course of history. Your actions can also help shape the future of the American Jewish community. The future of the Jewish experience in this country is in your hands.

I N D E X